Lead with Love

Lead with Love

A Revolutionary Approach to the Pro-Life Conversation
by Someone Who Has Overcome Abortion

Tori Shaw

RESOURCE *Publications* · Eugene, Oregon

Resource Publications
An Imprint of Wipf and Stock Publishers
199 W. 8th Ave., Suite 3
Eugene, OR 97401

www.wipfandstock.com

PAPERBACK ISBN: 978-1-6667-0784-7
HARDCOVER ISBN: 978-1-6667-0785-4
EBOOK ISBN: 978-1-6667-0786-1

03/02/22

For the Pro-Life Community,
Thank you for your passion and determination in the fight against abortion. It's my prayer that this book will provide valuable insight from someone who has experienced abortion. May this fresh approach be a blessing as you continue to do God's work.

To my family,
Thank you for your constant support and for always cheering me on. I could never adequately express my gratitude and love for each one of you.

Contents

Prologue

THROUGHOUT LAURA'S CHILDHOOD NO one discussed sex, pornography, sex-trafficking, or abortion. She had never even heard these topics mentioned until middle school. One day on the bus, one of her friends brought up the word abortion. She felt silly knowing so little about sex and having no idea what abortion was. As soon as she got home, she asked her mom what it meant. Her mother's eyes quickly darted away from Laura, and her facial expression became distorted. Laura knew instantly that her mom didn't want to discuss it and assumed she must strongly disagree with it. Laura explained that she had heard the word after school, so her mother told her that sometimes women decide they aren't ready for a baby, so they have an abortion to become unpregnant. Laura didn't press her mother any further; she knew it made her mom very uncomfortable.

That tiny bit of information about abortion appeased Laura and she tucked it into the back of her mind until the topic came up again, a few years later. This time she overheard a conversation by several Christian women at a local coffee shop. They called women who had abortions murderers, referred to the clinic as a "mill," and loudly voiced their disgust for any woman who might do such a thing. Suddenly, Laura had a new layer of information that wrapped around what her mother had quickly explained years earlier. What she thought was just a "procedure" that some women had when they didn't want to be pregnant, she now saw as shameful.

A couple of months later, one of her high school classmates confided in her and a small group of friends that she had just had an abortion. A few other girls chimed in and admitted that they had also gotten abortions.

Laura was confused. If abortion was such a terrible thing, why were so many girls her age going through with it. Her mind began to shift again about the topic. She began to think that maybe abortion is acceptable, at least in certain situations, but something no one openly admitted to, especially to those who believe it's wrong.

Laura began to listen more closely when she heard the word abortion. She wanted to hear what other people really thought. On the news, she saw groups shouting that abortion should be the woman's choice. It's her body, after all. It appeared to her that these groups were advocating for the rights of women and that a child would take those rights away. She observed other groups holding signs that said, "Abortion is murder," and "God hates baby-killers." They also yelled, seeming to only advocate for the life of the fetus. Neither group seemed very approachable but at least the pro-choice group desired the best for a woman in a tough situation. She wondered if God really did hate abortion. If so, she figured He probably hated anyone that had ever had an abortion or helped someone get one. She assumed He hated her too, since she wasn't sure she agreed with the loud pro-life protesters.

Social media proved to be a place where Laura could find all sorts of opinions on the matter. Those who posted about abortion were usually extremely pro-life or extremely pro-choice. The two extremes frustrated her. She wanted to develop her own thoughts about the topic but didn't feel comfortable talking to either group. She worried they would verbally attack her if her questions opposed their stance. Some of the pro-life posts said hateful things about women who had chosen abortion and others heaped shame and condemnation on anyone considering their options. The pro-choice posts encouraged freedom for women and a chance to be prepared before starting a family. She surmised that most women wanted freedom and a chance for a good future but couldn't understand why the pro-life advocates wouldn't also want that for women. None of the posts ever explained that.

Laura thought about the topic now and then but mostly, it never entered her mind. Until one night during her sophomore year of college as she looked at the pregnancy test, she had purchased at the drug store. The pink lines confirmed what she feared. She was pregnant. At only nineteen years old, she had no idea how to handle this unwanted news. She was a college student, didn't have much of a relationship with the guy that got her pregnant, and had just lost her part time job.

She didn't know what to do. She couldn't tell her mom. They never even had the "talk" when she was growing up. She had only been taught about sex in school or overheard things her friends were giggling about. Her mom didn't know she was sexually active and would be terribly disappointed in her. She considered getting the advice of her friends but then realized she didn't know where her friends stood on the issue and feared their harsh opinions. She knew that there were agencies in the community that could help single moms but wondered if they would belittle her for not being happy about the pregnancy.

Then she recalled all the posts about a woman's choice. She had never imagined she would find herself in this position, but now that freedom to choose seemed like a much better option. She figured, at least this way she wouldn't have to tell anyone. She could go on with college, as if it never happened. She didn't necessarily want to have the abortion, but she didn't believe anyone would really help her without also humiliating and condemning her for even considering abortion.

Laura made the appointment for the following week. She kept her pregnancy hidden from her roommates and friends, except one. She hadn't wanted to tell anyone, but she was required to have someone drive her home after the procedure, so she didn't have a choice. She chose to confide in an acquaintance that had multiple sexual partners. She figured this girl would empathize with her and wouldn't judge her. Each night her mind raced with worry and fear. She wasn't sure if this was the right choice, but she didn't know what else to do.

As her friend drove to the abortion facility in a neighboring town, Laura's mind was racing. She was torn. She was desperate. She was weary. They inched closer to the clinic and noticed protestors standing nearby. The nurse she had spoken with warned her about them, saying they were hateful and oppressive, but she had hoped they wouldn't be there. The pro-lifers were holding large signs with aborted fetuses on them and using bullhorns to get the attention of the people pulling into the parking lot. Laura wanted to hide. She feared what they might say to her. As they parked the car and climbed out, she heard someone yell that considering abortion is selfish and then, they called her a baby-killer. Another person shouted about God's hatred toward sinners, especially murderers. They obviously saw themselves as the "good guys" and viewed her as a disgusting, dirty sinner. Their huge, graphic signs seemed like a wall they had erected. The tone of their voice and their pious attitudes kept her from even making eye contact with them. Their words caused her to run as quickly as possible inside the clinic.

Once inside, Laura felt her tensed body finally relax. At least these people wouldn't judge her. As she went through with the procedure, she did her best to occupy her mind with other thoughts. She was already at the clinic now, so she assumed she had to go through with it. Where would she go anyway? Who would even want to help her?

When it was over, she was completely exhausted in every way possible. She dreaded walking out to the car. What would they say to her now? She didn't need to hear their judgmental opinions or their angry statements. But truthfully, she felt she deserved to be called every terrible name they could come up with. She knew what she had done was wrong. She regretted it already. A shroud of guilt and shame covered her, and she wanted to hide in her dorm room for the rest of her life.

Her friend drove as fast as she could past the glaring protestors. Laura couldn't make out their words as they drove by because she bent down in the front seat of the car and covered her head to avoid their stares.

She slept for what seemed like days and promised herself she would never tell anyone. She would do her best to forget it and pretend it never happened. This proved to be more difficult than she imagined but she persistently hid her overwhelming emotions. She avoided family and close friends because she thought they may be able to see through her fake smile. Over time, she learned to push the thoughts and feelings deep down and cover them up with alcohol and more promiscuous relationships. When the guilt or shame entered her mind, she quickly reminded herself of all the pro-choice arguments she had heard over the years, which allowed her to justify her decision. Then she scolded herself for even thinking about the abortion.

Over the next few years, she did her best to avoid any conversation that might bring up the topic. She knew hearing the opinions of others would only bring many difficult emotions to the surface. When she saw social media posts or news reports about abortion, she felt as if everyone around her could see the shroud of shame she had worn out of the abortion facility; the shroud she couldn't take off. She worried about the future, assuming God would punish her by never allowing her to have children or by taking them from her at an early age. She felt she deserved to be treated poorly because of the choice she made at nineteen, so she allowed others to abuse her emotionally and physically.

After college, Laura married a young man who introduced her to Jesus. This was not the hateful, cruel, harsh God she had been told about previously. This Lord, she was learning about, was full of love and compassion and joy. She desired a close relationship with Him but believed that God hated her because of her choice several years earlier. For the first time, she talked openly about the abortion. Her new husband was surprised by the news but assured her that God loved her and would forgive her if she asked Him to. Her husband didn't belittle her or assume her choice had been an easy one, just for convenience. She began to believe that God may actually love her, because of the unconditional love and kindness she saw in her husband. She believed that she could be forgiven, and soon she began a beautiful relationship with Jesus Christ.

Even though Laura was growing in her faith, she never spoke of her abortion. She continued to hide the secret because she feared what others might think, especially her Christian friends. She believed God had forgiven her but didn't believe His people would. She continued to run anytime the topic was brought up and never shared the truth about how abortion had harmed her. She spent twenty-five years never telling anyone other than her husband. She cringed at the thought of anyone else making the choice to abort but felt the stakes were too high to speak up.

Her mother received a cancer diagnosis when Laura was forty-four years old. The cancer had not been caught early and the prognosis wasn't good. One day, while Laura was sitting by her mother's bed, they talked softly about things from her childhood. Much to her surprise, her mother's eyes filled with tears, and she began to share something she had been hiding for almost fifty years. Laura could not believe her ears as she heard her mother speak about the child, she aborted a few years before Laura was born. Tears streamed down her face as she explained the situation she had been in when she found out she was pregnant and how horrific the abortion experience had been. She expressed her desire to keep the secret hidden because she thought no one would love her if they knew what she had done. She confessed to years and years of shame, depression, suicidal thoughts, self-harm, and self-loathing. She apologized profusely and begged Laura to forgive her for aborting her brother or sister.

Laura's mind couldn't make sense of what she was being told. If only her mom had explained what abortion was when she asked so many years earlier. If only her mom had been honest about the destructive impact abortion has on women and their families. If only her mom had not suffered her entire life with this dark, ugly secret. If only her mom had shared her story, Laura wouldn't have felt so alone and helpless, and maybe, just maybe she wouldn't have made the same devastating choice.

1

Why Things Must Change

OVER THE PAST COUPLE of years, I have become immersed in the pro-life movement, which has been a drastic change for me in many ways. I spent seventeen years desperately trying to avoid anyone who called themselves "pro-life." I avoided them, not because of their stance for life, but because of the way so many pro-life advocates shared their beliefs and opinions.

You see, I am a post-abortive woman. At sixteen years old, I discovered I was pregnant one day and aborted my child the next. When I left the abortion clinic on June 19, 1999, I went into hiding and stayed there for seventeen years following my abortion. You can read the story in full detail in my book, *I Had a Secret for Seventeen Years*.

I would have never considered myself "pro-choice" before my abortion but when I found myself in a terrible situation, abortion felt like the easy way out. That was, of course, a common lie that so many women believe. Since my choice in 1999, I have been against abortion because I experienced firsthand the impact that choice often has on a woman and have endured the very real loss of my child continually throughout the years. No one would have known my stance however, because I did everything I could to hide my abortion and keep my opinion to myself.

Shame was the main reason for my silence. Even as a believer in Jesus Christ, who knew I was forgiven, I could not escape the shame. I didn't feel condemned by the Father; I felt condemned by many believers and those calling themselves "pro-life."

For years I never talked about my abortion with anyone but if I had wanted to, I probably would have reached out to someone in the "pro-choice" movement first. After all, they didn't come across as judgmental or unreasonable. The thought of sharing my story with a pro-life person or organization caused a great deal of fear and anxiety within me. I knew God had forgiven me, but I believed anyone with a heart for the preborn would shame me, hate me, and ridicule me.

I decided to share my story for the first time with a friend who was brave enough to openly expose her secret. I felt safe enough to open up to her because I knew she wouldn't judge me. I knew she would understand. Even after completing a post-abortion Bible study with my friend, I was still too afraid to speak about my abortion or discuss my experience in general for many more years. I couldn't bear the thought of anyone knowing what I had done because it appeared post-abortive women were scorned and abhorred by the pro-life community.

In May of 2016, I finally emerged from hiding after surrendering to the Holy Spirit's call for me to release this secret and trust Him with it. Things haven't been the same since, in the best possible way. I live in freedom now. I am whole and full of life and love. I no longer care if others look at me with disdain. I founded Not Forgotten Ministries and have dedicated my life to helping women make a choice they won't regret and helping others find healing after abortion.

As I have ministered to ladies with an abortion in their past, it has become abundantly clear that the way I felt for seventeen years was not a unique experience. Every single woman I've encountered has felt the same shame and fear that I endured. During many of our Bible studies and group sessions, we have discussed the condemning, judgmental attitude portrayed by the pro-life community. The haughty way some pro-life advocates discuss abortion and sneer at post-abortive women, and those considering abortion, has caused so many of these ladies to hide their secret, try to deal with the trauma in silence, and never expose the truth of how abortion affected their lives.

One evening as we began a new post-abortion Bible study at my ministry office, a young lady shared that she had read an article about me. She had never heard anyone talk about abortion the way I did. She had been drawn to me because she knew I wouldn't judge her. She had decided to come out of hiding because she felt safe with me. Many times throughout the study, it was mentioned that if she hadn't come across that article, she would have never sought freedom in Christ because so many comments made by the pro-life community had caused her to believe that freedom wasn't available to her, and she wasn't deserving of a life without shame.

This young lady's openness about the pain she felt due to the abrasive attitudes, cavalier comments, and snobbish statements made by those who oppose abortion, broke my heart. God began to birth in me a desire to shed light on this issue and help those working so hard to save lives, better understand how they are, at times, a detriment to their own cause.

I know, without doubt, that most pro-life advocates have the best intentions and never intend to push anyone away or cause others to feel inferior or alienated. I also know, however, that the loudest voices within the pro-life movement are often hateful, negative, and condemning.

It is my sincere belief that women (and men) who have experienced abortion are the hidden key in the fight against abortion. I say hidden key, instead of missing key, because post-abortive women aren't missing. We are everywhere. According to Abort73.org, in 2019 alone, approximately 887,000 women had an abortion in the United States. [1] Assuming that many women have experienced an abortion every year since Roe vs. Wade in 1973, approximately 43,463,000 women are carrying around the burden of abortion.

There are women of all ages; those who had abortions forty years ago to those who had an abortion yesterday. These women have stories that need to be told. People who have firsthand experience with abortion are uniquely qualified to share the impact this "choice" has on women and families. Their stories will have an impact like none other. Post-abortive women can expose the truth of abortion and all that accompanies it. The ones who have struggled with choosing abortion, endured the pain of an abortion, and felt the shame that follows an abortion are the most qualified to relate to other post-abortive people, as well as those who are abortion-vulnerable.

> *People who have firsthand experience with abortion are uniquely qualified to share the impact this "choice" has on women and families.*

We must ask ourselves why the "key" in the fight against abortion is hiding. Why are they silent?

I believe it's because we, the pro-life movement, have silenced the most valuable weapon in our arsenal.

1. "Abortion Statistics." 2

Once God laid it upon my heart to write this book, I decided to conduct a survey among women who have experienced abortion. I shared an anonymous survey on social media and within one week there were one hundred forty responses. The responses were made by women who are now pro-life as well as those who still consider themselves pro-choice. I'd like to share the results from the survey with you.

A Closer Look: Post-Abortive Men and Women

140 women who have experienced abortion answered an anonymous questionnaire about their experience. (185 abortive babies are represented with these responses.)

Have you openly shared your abortion story?

- 14% are open about their abortions.
- 50% have only told one/two people or have never told anyone.
- 35% of those that have shared took a very long time to find the courage.

How long have you kept your secret?

- 60% have kept it a secret for more than 10 years
- 32% have kept it a secret for more than 20 years
- 13% have kept it a secret for more than 30 years

Do you believe the church (any denomination) is critical or judgmental of men or women who have chosen abortion?

- 80% said yes
- 20% said no

Do you believe the pro-life community is critical or judgmental of men or women who have chosen abortion?

- 59% said yes
- 41% said no

When you found out about your pregnancy, did you seek help from a pastor, church, or pro-life organization?

- 8% said yes
- 92% said no

Have you had any negative experiences with pro-life supporters?

- 57% said yes
- 43% said no

If someone considering an abortion asked for your advice, what would your answer be?

- 95% said, "don't do it, you'll regret it."
- Only four people out of 140 would give the advice to choose abortion.

Do you believe post-abortive men and women have dealt with the trauma appropriately?

- 91% said no
- 9% said yes

If you had heard the stories of post-abortive men and women, would you still have chosen abortion?

- 62% said no
- 10% said yes
- 27% said unsure
- Eighty-six people out of 140 said they would not have had an abortion if a post-abortive man or woman had shared their story with them.

What have you experienced post abortion?

- Shame—93%
- Guilt—95%
- Regret—89%
- Fear of God's Punishment—62%
- Depression—78%
- Anxiety/Panic Attacks—54%
- Numbness—49%
- Denial—45%
- Unexplained Anger/Rage—49%
- Self-loathing—59%

- Self-harm—27%
- Self-medicating (drugs, alcohol, etc.)—46%
- Avoiding pregnant women or children—27%
- Avoiding conversations discussing the topic of abortions—54%
- Inability to forgive yourself or others—67%
- Feelings of Isolation—50%
- Fear of losing living children or future children—48%
- Low self-esteem/poor self-image/no confidence—61%
- Preoccupation with replacing the aborted child—19%
- Nightmares/Flashbacks—39%
- Suicidal thoughts/Suicide attempts—34%

If men and women with an abortion in their past opened up about their experiences, do you think it would have an impact on others?

- Only one person out of 140 people said it would *not* have impact.

  What kind of impact would it have?

- 55% said it would reveal the truth about abortion.
- 60% said it would make women think more before choosing to abort.
- 58% said it would encourage other people who have dealt with abortion to open up about their abortions.
- 57% said it would change the opinion about our abortion in our country.
- 53% said it would help pro-life advocates better understand how to talk to post-abortive people.

  If you could go back now, would still choose abortion?

- 87% said no
- Only eighteen out of 140 people said they might still choose abortion.

The questionnaire responses didn't surprise me but seeing on paper what I knew to be true, had an impact on me. Something must change in this fight for life. This book will explain why change is needed and offer proven strategies for implementing that change.

Lead with Love is designed to expose the issues that have damaged our fight for life and provide insight on how to turn things around. We share respectful and loving techniques for communicating with someone who has an abortion in their past, minister to someone considering abortion, as well discuss the topic of abortion in general.

> *86 people out of 140 said they would not have had an abortion if a post-abortive woman had shared their story with them.*

As you read, it is my prayer that you will feel the magnitude of this issue. I pray that you will understand the impact for life that is possible if we, the pro-life movement, embrace a Christ-like approach in the fight against abortion. If we seek God's help and lead with love, women and families will find healing after abortion, the truth about abortion will be exposed, lives will be saved, and the cycle will be broken.

2

How Did We Get Here?

To best correct an issue, I believe it's important to learn as much as we can about the problems we face and acknowledge where they originated. I've paid close attention over the past few years, which caused me to ask myself, "How did we get here?" It didn't take long for me to recognize four matters that have negatively impacted our fight against abortion.

While I know there are many pro-life advocates that are not Christians, the words within the pages of this book will undoubtedly speak loudest to those who are believers in Jesus Christ. That's because the lens with which I view the world is based upon my belief that God is the Creator of each and every human life. Even if you do not agree with my beliefs, I encourage you to continue reading; much of this book will provide insight on how to best fight for the lives of the preborn.

Blindness is More Common Than We Think

While physical blindness is easy to recognize, emotional and spiritual blindness are not. Sadly, there are many people walking around completely blind to an assortment of things. Many are naïve to the truth about abortion and/or its effects on women and families. Most could never guess how many abortions are performed each day in America, let alone the world. While a lot of people know what the term abortion means, very few actually understand the details of what happens during the various abortion procedures.

For a lot of these individuals, I believe the adage "ignorance is bliss," is appropriate. For others, they simply believe what they're told by pro-choice groups, public school systems, media, and other influential people within their communities. These days, it can be rare for people to research topics to develop their own opinions.

Women are especially "duped" by organizations like Planned Parenthood and by much of the media. We are told that abortion is healthcare, a fetus isn't a human, terminating a child is often in the best interest of the child and/or the mother, abortion procedures are safe and rare, and even that post-abortion issues aren't a reality. Any other traumatic event would be dealt with in a compassionate, therapeutic, caring way. Abortion isn't. That may be because our culture doesn't view abortion as a traumatic event, even though many women with an abortion in their past say their experience was much like being raped. These procedures can be extremely traumatic, but our society drives women to struggle all alone with a multitude of symptoms connected with post-traumatic stress disorder. Symptoms that include, shame, guilt, suicidal thoughts and attempts, fear, anxiety, depression, flashbacks, nightmares, substance abuse, social isolation, etc.

Our culture boldly says, "My body, my choice," while arguing that a woman should be able to do whatever she wants with her body. One might wonder then, why it is a crime to be a prostitute or drive while intoxicated? Maybe it's because those actions could affect other people. The pro-abortion community seems to forget that abortion does also. With every abortion, the life of someone else is either ended or severely damaged. Shockingly, our society has even turned a blind eye to proof that exposes the selling of fetal body parts.

One of the two contemporary political parties in the United States say they are "pro-person." Even that wording is deceptive. Doesn't it seem like a "pro-person" party would also be a pro-life party? Individuals that do not read between the lines would support this political party because they care about people, right? In truth, this party supports the termination of persons up to birth and claims that the procedure has zero negative consequences for the women who choose it. If a group calls themselves "pro-person," it seems they would care for the most vulnerable persons as well as the men and women abortion affects.

It's said that abortion is rare and that women don't realize they are ending a life. Sadly, however, some women are fully aware that they are carrying a life within their wombs. Yet, they are proudly pro-choice. Some even say taking a life through abortion is not a big deal or even find it comical.

However, even one of the most important United States of America documents, The Declaration of Independence, says otherwise. It states, "We hold these truths to be self-evident, that all men are created equal, that they are endowed by their Creator with certain unalienable Rights, that among these are life, liberty and the pursuit of happiness."[1] In America we are all endowed certain unalienable rights, including life. So why it is it acceptable to end the life of the tiniest Americans? Are they not being denied an unalienable right?

Some media outlets go as far as to tell us abortion is love when, in reality, abortion is quite the opposite. It demonstrates that violence will get us out of an unwanted situation and is the best way for women to reach their goals. If the abortion industry truly cared for women, they would provide more than a quick fix for an unwanted pregnancy. They would empower women in crisis by calling out their strengths and reminding them that they don't have to end the life of their child to be successful. They would help women understand all the options available to them and even point them to places that could offer help such as pregnancy resource centers. They would validate the pain many women feel after an abortion and offer counseling and support to help these women.

I've been told that an abortion recovery room is the saddest place on earth. Even the women who are proud of their choice to abort, are typically enveloped with sadness, shame, and a broken heart while lying in that recovery chair. All these women are rushed out of the door when their allotted time is up. They are forced to go home and deal with all their emotions alone. And since abortion is a "right" they chose, they often feel they do not deserve to grieve or be sorrowful. So, they shove all their emotions deep down as quickly as they can and try to pretend like nothing happened. If the abortion industry really cared for and loved women, none of this would be happening.

The pro-abortion community acts as if abortion has no consequences and is every woman's right. If that's true, why do so many women who have had an abortion remain silent? Why are they hiding? I believe it's because many who have experienced abortion know there are very real consequences and they've realized they were manipulated into believing that this so-called "right," would be best for them.

Deception on a grand scale is at the heart of the abortion issue. We are deceived by pro-abortion organizations, pro-abortion advocates, and

---

1. Jefferson, Declaration of Independence. Preamble.

much of the media, but we are also affected by deception of a different kind. The Bible says we have an enemy who is also called the Father of Lies (John 8:44 ESV). It is Satan's goal to deceive people on a multitude of levels. We are called to be light to the world around us (Matthew 5:14–16 NIV) but the handy work by the Father of Lies has influenced our culture so that it does not value light. We have become so accustomed to darkness; we think it provides safety. People often build up walls to keep the light out because light will expose the truth and force them to deal with their choices and opinions. These walls are extremely difficult to break through.

> "Satan, who is the god of this world, has blinded the minds of those who don't believe." 2 Corinthians 4:4a (NLT)

I remember a time when I was blind to many things. When I look back now, I cannot believe how narrow-minded and clueless I was. I was simply unable to see clearly. The same is true for so many in our world today. They may be well educated, done their research, and feel like an expert on the topic. They may even be in church every week and lead a Bible study, but until God causes the scales to fall from their eyes, they will never see things clearly. The good news: is it can happen! Just like the scales fell from Saul's eyes in Acts 9:18 (NIV), God can cause scales to fall from the eyes of our family, friends, neighbors, and co-workers. Let's not forget what became of Saul! He became Paul! He went from killing Christians to spreading the gospel! This type of amazing turn-around is still possible because our God is the same today as He was when Paul lived.

Those who are blind to the truth about abortion, need our prayers. No matter what we say, how we act, or what we do, they will never see clearly without God intervening!

Negative Overtakes Positive

Have you ever heard the expression, "One bad apple ruins the bunch?" That saying explains another on-going issue in our fight against abortion. While there are tons of passionate, life-affirming, God-honoring, pro-life advocates, there are also those who have good intentions but often cause more harm than good.

I believe whole-heartedly that almost everyone in the pro-life movement wants to save babies and believes what they are saying and/or doing is helping achieve that goal. The problem is, many are so caught up in their judgements of other people, that they aren't helping the way they desire to.

For example, imagine a terribly nervous young woman pulling into the abortion clinic parking lot is greeted by a sign with an aborted baby pictured and hears an advocate yelling, "What you're doing is selfish! You are nothing but a murderer!" Chances are, she's going to run as quickly as possible inside the clinic doors because at least they say they offer non-judgmental support.

The advocate in that situation did speak truth; abortion is often a selfish act, and it does end someone's life. However, the advocate pushed the young woman away with their harsh words and loud tone. The picture on the sign was relevant and would be a good tool in the right environment but holding it placed a barrier between them and the woman, a barricade that kept them from saving the baby she carried.

There are some in the movement that may disagree with me. Some people believe that yelling hateful comments, condemning women, passing judgement, calling out the sins of the others, and carrying graphic signs is the best way to fight against abortion. If that is a stance you've held, I encourage you to consider the difference between being effective and simply being right. As pro-life advocates, we are right and many of us really want others to know how right we are. We must realize that just being right isn't helping our cause. To be effective, we must be willing to gently speak truth so that a mother is willing to talk to us further. If she feels judged or condemned, she will run into the clinic. If we are kind and loving, offering help and hope to the mother and she willingly receives it, the baby comes along with her.

Asserting our point of view and demanding others agree with us will never be effective. We should never compromise our beliefs or condone abortion in any way. But isn't it better to do our job effectively rather than to stubbornly stand our ground, if it means the lives of babies and mommas can be saved?

Now imagine there were also seven additional, very calm, loving, pro-life advocates standing on the sidewalk that day. Chances are that the young mother didn't even notice them because the loud, accusatory, angry voice monopolized the atmosphere. Even if she did see the smiling advocates, and had the desire to speak with them, she would most likely be too afraid to walk in their direction because of the person yelling at her. It would feel much safer inside the clinic.

It's important to remember that as Christians, we are called to be the hands and feet of Jesus. If we are hostile with our hands and feet, and hateful with our words, we will be pushing those we are supposed to be serving, away from Jesus.

I think it's also necessary to point out the many disagreements and spats amongst groups within the pro-life community. We are all on the same team. We all want the same thing. However, pride, competitiveness, jealously, etc. are tools used by Satan to divide us. The enemy wants to bring our momentum to a halt. What better way than to bring discord among the very ones who could have the most impact? The amount of good that could come from working together is unquantifiable, but the negativity occurring among these groups tends to outweigh so much of the positive.

The idea that negative overtakes positive is true in many situations. Think about a time when you were given corrective criticism. Do you remember the compliments they gave also, or just the criticism? For me, I almost always remember the words I didn't like hearing, even if several nice things were also said. It often doesn't matter how many positive things were mentioned about the work we did or the role we played, when someone criticizes us, our minds tend to focus almost solely on the negative.

The same can happen in relationships. We may think we know a friend or co-worker but then something is said or done that makes us question it all. Even if we've gotten along for ten years and worked well together through many seasons, if that person is suddenly selfish, cruel, or bossy, something changes. The negative overtakes the positive.

The topic of abortion can be a tricky conversation to have with someone, especially if you do not know their stance on it. This is one of those things that can end up ruining a relationship, as mentioned above. It's not typically what pro-lifers believe that causes division, it's the way they share those beliefs.

A pro-abortion friend once told me she had never heard someone speak about abortion with gentleness. She had overheard heated discussions, seen in-your-face social media posts, and been talked down to by those in the pro-life movement, but had never had a calm, civil discussion with someone about the topic. Therefore, she spent years not truly hearing what the advocates had to say because she was bombarded by the loud, sarcastic, judgmental voices of those who didn't agree with her. Even if she had wanted to ask questions or get input from a pro-life friend, she would have chosen not to because of all the hateful things she had heard and seen. After several gentle, calm, considerate discussions with me, she changed her mind about abortion and has joined me in the fight for life.

Being passionate in this fight is a beautiful thing but we must carefully consider our words and actions when discussing this topic, even when it's with someone on the same team as we are, because we never know who is listening or how our words could be impacting the stance they take. Our negative conversations and belittling social media posts can overtake all our positive intentions.

As believers fighting against abortion, we are primed and ready to make a difference, but if we are looking down on others, we cannot also be humble enough to be used by the Holy Spirit. We must pray for grace and gentleness as we navigate this path. It's easy to wonder how someone could possibly choose to kill their own child or to contemplate how terrible a person must be in order to perform abortions. In these cases, however, we too are allowing negative to overtake the positive. These are people, just like you and me, who are making a mistake, just like you and I have. God sees all their beauty because He created them and loves them. He does not like their choices and wants more for their lives, but He still loves them. When we only look at the negative in another person, even an abortionist or a woman getting her eleventh abortion, we are being judgmental and cannot be used in that person's life.

> Our negative conversations and belitting social media posts can overtake all of our positive intentions.

Anyone who has experienced shame knows that it has a great deal of power. The enemy uses shame to keep us quiet, paralyze us, and stall our growth. Shame will keep a woman from sharing her abortion story for thirty years, even though doing so would bring freedom into her life and be blessing to others. Shame is so negative that, in a woman's mind, it cancels out all the positives.

Our culture encourages individuals and groups to loudly share their point of view, without concern of offending others or hurting someone in the process. Many times, thoughts and ideas are shoved down our throats, so to speak. Some in the pro-life movement have taken this approach as well, often trying to speak the truth and then earn the trust of those who need to hear it most. Jesus did the opposite of that. He earned the trust of others by loving them (even the sinners), without ever compromising *the* truth. Then, He said what needed to be said which led them to the Father. Jesus led with love.

Being positive attracts people, while being negative repels them. That's true for life in general. We all know someone who finds the negative in every situation. It can feel draining to be around a person like that. My family lovingly jokes, "Don't be a Debbie-Downer," when someone is being negative. We say that to gently remind one another that negativity breads negativity and isn't going to help any situation. However, someone that lives from a place of positivity and joy, draws people in. We want to be around those who find beauty in all circumstances because joy and gratitude are contagious and our souls crave that, whether we realize it or not.

It's tempting for us to negatively react to situations that occur, but as individuals and groups, it's important for us to remain positive, even in negative circumstances. I once heard a pastor say, we should all desire to be more like a thermostat rather than a thermometer. A thermometer is a device for determining temperature. A thermostat is a device that regulates the temperature. In this crazy world we're living in, as Christians, we should be like a thermostat. We should be regulating the atmosphere around us, not reacting to it. That's easier said than done but, nonetheless, it should be our prayer that God would enable us to control our emotions and keep our eyes on Him. We should also consider that a thermometer reflects what's happening around it by showing the current temperature. A thermostat, however, has the power to change it. If it is hot in my home, I use my thermostat to turn on the air conditioner make it cooler. The same is true when it's cold in my home. I use the thermostat to change the environment and make it warmer. Not only should we be constant when the atmosphere around us is changing, we should also be influencing our environment, making it warmer or colder when needed. God's grace will empower us to be the influence our environment needs. Instead of changing with the climate, *we can change* the climate. That will only happen when we we're positive and approachable.

In the pro-life movement, negativity has overtaken so many of the positive things we have done and are currently doing. Outsiders focus on the negative, ugly, loud things that have surrounded the movement therefore, many people refuse to hear anything from a group they have deemed judgmental and hateful. And that isn't helping anyone.

The Church and Home-Life Have Failed Us

Let me first share how much I love the Church! It is so much more than a building. The Church has played a tremendous role in my walk with Christ. My family has been loved on and prayed for by the church. I've been able to use my gifts and talents as a member of the Church and have abundantly blessed by the gifts and talents of others over the years.

God's design for the church is beautiful. In the New Testament, Church is discussed over one hundred times. The Greek word used in the Bible is *ecclesia*. This term is formed from two words which mean, "assembly" and "to call out" or "the called-out ones." That definition reveals that the Church is a body of believers that have been called out by God, away from the world, to live under His authority. These called-out believers are also called the Body of Christ (1 Corinthians 12:12–27 NIV). The Church, on a local level and as one unified entity, is the primary vehicle with which God carries out His purposes. Through us, the Body of Christ, God makes Himself known throughout the world.

The Church is the most powerful force on earth when we allow it to be. However, the Church in general has not played that role in the fight against abortion. Although the Church has been called out to be different than the world around us, the differences are often hard to see.

> "Do not love the world or anything in the world. If anyone loves
> the world, love of the Father is not in them." 1 John 2:15(NIV)

Anything that is not of God is of the world. In today's world, many churches look no different than the world. Many congregations have even begun condoning things that the Bible explicitly condemns. More often though, the Church remains silent about issues that should boldly separate us from the world. Abortion is one of those issues, along with homosexuality, adultery, pornography, etc. These topics should be taught from the pulpit and in youth groups in every congregation of believers throughout the world, but they rarely are.

As the Executive Director of a pro-life ministry, I have been shocked by the lack of involvement by churches in my community. We've had a nearby church return a newsletter by mail, asking us to remove them from our mailing list. We've requested opportunities to share about our ministry in numerous churches in our area, only to find that many do not want the topic discussed in their building. There are many denominations that encourage the right to abortion as well, which makes them an obstacle in the fight for life.

I have not been told the reasons these church families support abortion, but I imagine it must break the Father's heart. The Bible is clear that life is precious to God, from the womb to the tomb, as expressed in the following verses:

> "From birth I was cast on you; from my mother's womb you have been my God." Psalm 22:10 (NIV)

> The word of the Lord came to me, saying, 'Before I formed you in the womb, I knew you, and before you were born, I consecrated you; I appointed you a prophet to the nations.'" Jeremiah 1:4–5 (NIV)"

> "For you created my inmost being, you knit me together in my mother's womb. I praise you because I am fearfully and wonderfully made; your works are wonderful; I know that full well. My frame was not hidden from you when I was made in the secret place, when I was woven together in the depths of the earth. Your eyes saw my unformed body; all the days ordained for me were written in your book before one of them came to be." Psalm 139:13–16 (NIV)

Every single human life is created by God and should be treated with respect, not because of the circumstances they were conceived in but because life itself is a miracle. It's hard for me to understand why a Bible-believing, Christ-serving church family would not agree with that. The same is true with other important topics. It seems some churches pick and choose what they want to believe from the Bible, which causes them to look a lot like the world around them.

On the other hand, some churches go to an extreme when it comes to fighting for life. They can often be very hurtful toward someone who is pregnant out of wedlock, has had an abortion, or is considering one. About ten years ago, a church on the outskirts of the town I grew up in discovered that a student in their youth group was pregnant. When the church Elders heard the news, they forced the young lady to stand up in front of the entire church family, explain her situation, confess her sin, and beg the congregation for forgiveness. This was a staunchly pro-life church, but the requirements forced upon the teenager, caused her to run to the abortion clinic the following day. The experience heaped shame and condemnation upon her, which caused her to abort her baby and become suicidal. She also never returned to any church, to my knowledge. I can't imagine how hurt she must have been. She was harmed and shamed by those that should have loved her the most, regardless of the situation, just because they are supposed to love like Jesus. In this case, the church family was different than the world but not in a way that draws people to Jesus. In fact, most nonbelievers would be appalled to find she was treated in such a demeaning way. It's not hard to understand why she would run from the representatives of God that showed her such little grace and mercy.

All Christians, regardless of church denomination, should be showing the world that Christ-followers are different because of our love for God and all His children. We must remember that we are concerned for the souls of the lost and the lives of the preborn, not just pointing out the sins of others. God doesn't need us, but He chooses to use us to minister to one another. Therefore, many times, the ministry of God only goes as far as the love of His people.

The church does not exist just to simply tell others what they are doing is wrong. It exists to help others make the choice that is right.

If that young girl or any of her friends got pregnant again, do you think they would go to the church for help? No! They would be scared to death for anyone to find out. They would fear having to expose their secrets in front of hundreds of accusatory, judgmental stares. Chances are, they would go straight to an abortion clinic to "take care of the problem." Jesus would not have put that young girl, or any sinner, in that position. In fact, Jesus often did more to offend the religious and love the sinners. Shouldn't His Church be following in His footsteps?

Many Christians assume that women having abortions aren't church goers. According to an article by Care Net, "Many women with unplanned pregnancies go silently from the church pew to the abortion clinic, convinced the church would gossip rather than help." [2] Sadly, "more than four in ten women who have had an abortion were church-goers when they ended the pregnancy," according to the study. This research proves that many churches are so focused on rebuking the sin, they forget to show love and grace to the sinners. Often the verbiage used when discussing abortion, if it's discussed at all, demeans anyone that might consider it and causes women who become pregnant or have had abortions to hide what they've done.

Churches who are unashamedly pro-life and whose pastors have the courage to speak the truth about the hot topics, also need to validate the sanctity of human life, from conception to natural death, and be clear about

2. Green, Women Go Silently. 1

why abortion is wrong. This needs to be done often and in numerous age-appropriate ways, so that everyone is clearly taught how valuable life is at every stage. The lack of this type of education and awareness has resulted in generations of Christians who aren't sure what they think about abortion.

As children grow up in the church, it's important for them to be taught how much God cares about them. Before they were even conceived, He dreamed up their existence. While in their mother's womb, He created them and designed a beautiful, purposeful life for them.

I attended church as a child but unfortunately, I learned very little about the things that truly matter. I did memorize all the books of the Bible in order, and while every single book in the Bible is important, knowing the names of them didn't teach me that I could have a relationship with the One who created me. It also didn't teach me that my identity should be found in God.

There is a huge difference between knowing about God and truly knowing Him. Even Satan believes there is a God. Our little ones need to be taught so much more than about His existence, they need to know who God is and how He feels about each of them. Knowing God and believing what He says about us will change everything.

If our children know the Creator, believe He created them and others on purpose, with a purpose, they will automatically have a firm belief in the sanctity of human life. That will be a beautiful foundation to build upon as we raise the next pro-life generation.

It's tempting to believe our children are getting all they need in church if they attend regularly but the truth is, even if our kids go to an amazing church every Sunday and Wednesday throughout the year, they are only being ministered to about 104 hours each year. Compare that to the 8,656 hours they are spending away from church each year. With numbers like that, parents must be intentional about pointing their children to Jesus, praying together as a family, studying the Bible, discussing the hard topics, modeling bold faith, worshiping together, attending church, memorizing scripture, and serving those around us. Notice that church is only one of the items in that list. As their parents, the rest is up to us.

Home-life has failed in this area for many of us. Don't get me wrong, I am fully aware that life is busy and chaotic, and the days seem to fly by. I'm pointing no fingers because my husband and I are currently raising four children of our own. I would love to say we're pros at all of this, but there is always room for improvement.

In addition to leading our children to the Heavenly Father, we need to discuss the hard topics like sex, drugs, alcohol, abuse, abortion, homosexuality, and many others. How will our children know the way to respond when someone offers them a beer, if we don't teach them? How will they know purity is desirable and protects them from a multitude of diseases, if we don't talk about it? The world never stops talking about these things. Without doubt, your child will hear about sex from a friend or through the health curriculum in his school, so we must be proactive, teaching them truth to combat all the lies heard in the community.

When I found out I was pregnant at sixteen years old, I knew what the word abortion meant, but I had never discussed it with anyone. I had no idea what really happens during a procedure designed to terminate a pregnancy. I had never heard anyone share their beliefs about why abortion was wrong. Deep in my gut I knew it was wrong, but I had nothing to back that feeling up with, so the excuses easily won the debate within me.

> If there is a topic that makes you feel uncomfortable when you talk about it with your child, it probably needs to be talked about often.

If there is a topic that makes you feel uncomfortable when you talk about it with your child, it probably needs to be talked about often. Discussing these awkward issues will become easier over time and I believe, every bit of discomfort is worth it if it allows our children to know they can come talk to us about anything.

The generations of parents that have passed without discussing these things, did a disservice to their children. Though most likely unintentional, their home life failed them in this area.

Weaponized Truth

What do you think most non-believers would say about Christians? There are a couple of words that immediately come to mind for me. Those words are judgmental and hypocritical.

This could be because there are many among us who call themselves Christians but do not live out the faith they claim to have.

(2 Timothy 3:5 ESV) It also may simply be because we are all sinners, even those who believe in Jesus. We still mess up, we still struggle with the ups and downs of life, and we still need grace daily.

For some reason, however, many Christ-followers forget their desperate need for a Savior. They forget they too were once lost. They get amnesia about the things they've said and done, and then begin pointing fingers at those who are standing in the place they once stood. This finger-pointing looks a lot like judgement and hypocrisy, doesn't it?

> "Walk in the wisdom of God as you live before the unbelievers and make it your duty to make Him known. Let every word you speak be drenched with grace and tempered with truth and clarity. For then you will be prepared to give a respectful answer to anyone who asks about your faith." Colossians 4:5–6 (TPT)

It's important for our conversations to be filled with love and grace. Whether with a family member or a stranger, we mustn't forget the power of our words.

> Kind words heal and help; cutting words wound and maim. Proverbs 15:4 (MSG)

Even when we're sure we know the truth and watching others around us go against that truth makes us angry, we are called to love them. (John 15:12 ESV). When we use the truth to condemn others and point out their flaws, I believe we are weaponizing truth.

Sadly, weaponizing truth has become the norm for some people within the pro-life movement and in the Body of Christ as a whole. The enemy loves this tactic and uses it to his advantage repeatedly. As Christ-followers, we must remember that being right, doesn't give us permission to be unkind.

Our beliefs do not make us better people. It's what we do with those beliefs that makes a difference. We do not need to perform to be in good standing with God, but if we are walking closely with the Father, being judgmental of others and weaponizing His truths will feel foreign to us. In fact, telling the truth in a hateful way will be counterproductive because the God of all Truth instructs us to love others and show them compassion.

> "Get rid of all bitterness, rage and anger, brawling and slander, along with every form of malice. Be kind and compassionate to one another, forgiving each other, just as in Christ God forgave you." Ephesians 4:31–32 (NIV)

Shaming to repentance is another strategy often used in the pro-life movement that causes more harm than good. A good example of this is calling women murderers or carrying signs that tell her she's going to hell. Heaping shame on someone considering abortion causes her to run inside the clinic. It also pushes post-abortive women further and further away from healing. Why would anyone want to come out of hiding, to speak up about the horrible truth of abortion, while the pro-life community is calling them names?

It should be noted that most post-abortive women know what they did was wrong. Pointing it out repeatedly does not point them to the One that forgives, redeems, and restores. They do not need to hear our judgments or opinions to figure out that they failed. Most live in a constant state of regret and shame, so we must be careful that our words and actions do not cause them to believe that God could never forgive them. Jesus' death on the cross was for all of us, even the post-abortive woman. There was no sign above Jesus that said, "This is for all sin—except abortion." As those already forgiven, we need to lead them to the cross, not cause them to fear it.

Even those who see nothing wrong with abortion aren't suddenly going to change their opinion because we yelled something cruel at them. Very few people get judged into life-change, but there are many who get loved into becoming a new creation. (2 Corinthians 5:17 NIV)

We should not view those who are pro-choice, those who work in the abortion industry, those who are considering abortions, or those who have had one as our adversaries. If we do, we will never have the compassion needed to help them.

Those facing an unplanned pregnancy need to feel safety with pro-life advocates. If we want them to choose life, they must feel loved by us, not hated. Using truth as a weapon does not create a safe, loving environment.

We are not called to abandon truth. After all, the truth sets us and others free. (John 8:32 NIV) We should speak truth without compromise but *with* compassion and love.

3

How Do We Change It?

Perspectives

TO CHANGE THE DIRECTION the pro-life movement is headed, and hopefully repair some of the damage that's been done, we must change our perspectives. We've spent far too long unknowingly looking down upon those who have had an abortion, those who may be considering abortion, and those who participate in performing abortions. It's almost as if there has been a blind spot that has limited our awareness. It's time to expose the darkness. It's time for truth to fully be revealed.

Of course, we want the truth about abortion exposed. Everything from when life begins to the emotional effects abortion has, must be brought to light. There is something else that needs to be exposed, however. Something that is equally important for those who already understand the value of human life and the tragedy abortion truly is.

Have you ever laid in bed at night and watched the moonlight sneak in through the window? Especially as children, those shifting shadows can seem frightening. As the light fades, the darkness begins to overtake the room. As I was watching the shadows in my room one night, I had an epiphany. Even though that scene was ominous, and it felt like the darkness was caving in on me, the light was responsible for the shifting shadows. It wasn't darkness overcoming the light, causing it to bend and sway. It was, in fact, the exact opposite of that. It was the light, overcoming the darkness!

As I let myself ponder that reality, I noticed that the shadows made by mingling tree limbs were only visible to me because of the light behind them. As the moon moved, so did the look of the shadows. The same is true with so many things in life. The way things appear to us is greatly affected by the perspective we have. A perspective that focuses on ourselves and our lifestyle, morals, and experience often cause us to look down on everyone that thinks differently than we do or makes choices we wouldn't make. It's very easy for us to slip into this perspective, without even realizing it. Darkness always breeds more darkness, whether we realize it or not.

I think it's important to consider this question, "When did God tell us to hatefully point out the sin of others?" The answer is—He didn't. He did say, however, to make one another aware of our sins in a loving manner. He told us to tell the truth in love.

With a self-focused, pious perspective, we will judge others and hatefully call out their sin without even realizing the consequences that may follow. That's why, to make a difference in our culture and cause positive change within the pro-life movement, we must look closely at our perspectives.

As Believers in Jesus Christ, our primary citizenship is the kingdom of heaven. It's time for all of us to act like it *and* think like it. Doing so will affect the perspective with which we view the world around us. As citizens of Heaven, abortion is something we should be fighting against because abortion is not of God. This makes abortion is a Kingdom issue, not merely a political one.

There are many perspectives or lenses, in which we view the world. Often our default lens is the "It's all about me lens." At times, we also look through a political lens, religious lens, race lens, victim lens, or sexuality lens, among others. The lens we need to focus on looking through is the kingdom lens. This lens enables us to see people the way God does. With this perspective, we will see inconveniences as opportunities and haters as someone who needs Jesus. We will also view ourselves differently with the kingdom lens. We will know our purpose and walk in it confidently. The best way to keep this perspective is to draw near to Jesus and find our identity in Him alone.

If we keep our eyes on Jesus, He will light up our path and we will not walk in darkness. (John 8:12 ESV) Knowing God results in every other kind of understanding. (Proverbs 9:10 NIV) Remembering that this is not our home, keeping our eyes on Jesus, and intentionally looking at others through the kingdom lens has the potential to change everything for us. Asking God to help us see things the way He does will produce love for those around us, regardless of who they are or what they've done.

Another aspect of living with a kingdom perspective is to remember that God is in control, and He does not turn a blind eye to wrongdoing. It is tempting to think we need to manage things ourselves or that God somehow needs our help. But God is the One who deals with those who do wrong. We are not called to dish out consequences or hatefully call out sin. We are called to pray and to love. God is the judge, we are not.

Yielding to the Father and remembering that He can do in moments what might take us years to do on our own, will help us maintain the kingdom perspective and remain humble. It's also vital for us not to forget that we were once lost and blind. We have been brought from darkness to light, but I believe it's important that we never forget where we came from. Being in the light doesn't make us better than those who are still in darkness, it just makes us blessed. If not for the grace of God, we would still be in the dark.

I have heard so many post-abortive women say they always considered themselves pro-life *until* they faced a crisis pregnancy of their own. Most of them say they were totally opposed to the idea of abortion, but when it was no longer just an abstract idea, things changed for them. That's why it is imperative for us to look at women considering abortion through a kingdom lens and put ourselves in their shoes. This can be accomplished by truly pondering what life would be like if you were in their exact scenario. That's impossible to do through a self-focused lens because we will look at them but keep our biases in place, which will not be beneficial. We must also put ourselves in the shoes of those who have had an abortion, remembering that for most of them, abortion was something they never imagined themselves doing. Most of them regret it terribly and wouldn't make the same choice again. Additionally, so many of these women are completely different people than they were the day they aborted their child. Their lives have changed in a million ways therefore, their character shouldn't be judged by a decision they made in the middle of a crisis. Would you want your character to be judged by a stupid decision you made years ago?

When we have a kingdom perspective, we will also be fully aware of the enemy and his schemes. The Bible says we are fighting a battle, not of flesh and blood, but a spiritual one. (Ephesians 6:12 NIV) As God's children, we must realize that our enemy wants to prevent us from achieving the purpose God has for us. It's time for us to know the power we have with the indwelling of the Holy Spirit. It's time for us to use that power to rebuke the enemy and all the plans he has orchestrated against us and against our ministries.

The Victims

Remembering who our fight is truly against will allow us to realize the preborn are not the only victims of abortion –the women and families involved are victims, too. Sin makes us all victims. Even sin *we* choose opens *us* up to Satan's power. We can easily become his victims, too. So, we must not view those who are considering abortion or those who have had one as our adversaries. We are not in agreement with their choices, but they are still children of God Almighty and it is our responsibility to treat them as such.

Christians are supposed to talk and walk differently than the world, so that means we should treat others differently too, with kindness and gentleness, even those we disagree with. We cannot judge others or decide how we will treat them based on their personalities, looks, or choices.

As those fighting against abortion, we are fighting for the helpless, voiceless lives of the preborn but we cannot forget, in order to save the baby, we must love the mom. Loving those who seem unlovable can feel like an impossible task. It is helpful to intentionally acknowledge the realities of why someone might end up in the clinic or why someone may have chosen abortion in the past.

Typically, women considering abortion are up against what they deem as an impossible situation. They feel hopeless like they have no other option. Difficult circumstances, relationship troubles, financial concerns, future plans, and a slew of other issues often cause an unplanned pregnancy to feel like the worst news possible. Abortion is sold as a solution; a "so-called" resolution to their problem.

There are also women who have been told by doctors and other professionals that abortion is the best choice based on the health of the mother or child. Pro-life doctors agree that because of medical advancements and modern technology, there is never a legitimate medical reason to abort a child. But when a scared young couple hears from "trusted" doctors that the pregnancy could cause serious risks to the mother's health and possibly lead to death, they often trust that abortion is the better option.

> *As those fighting against abortion, we are fighting for the helpless, voiceless lives of the preborn but we cannot forget, in order to save the baby, we must love the mom.*

When a couple, even with a planned pregnancy, are told that their baby will not be viable and are encouraged to end the pregnancy instead of pro-longing the inevitable, many are so heartbroken, they just follow the instructions of those who are supposedly looking out for their best interest. Too many times, those tests and opinions about a baby are wrong and a healthy baby could be aborted. The families that chose abortion, even at the advice of medical experts, often spend years worrying that they made the wrong choice, wondering if their situation would have really ended up as predicted. Other times, however, a baby does only live a few hours, but parents who choose life are so grateful for those moments with their baby. Doctors who talk their patients into abortion in these scenarios, are robbing these families of those precious moments. There are also times when a baby is still born. This is tragic for a family but a least they know they did not end the life of their child; it was a natural part of the pregnancy.

Rape is another delicate issue because of the trauma endured. It's often suggested that a pregnancy resulting from rape should be terminated. For the mothers who've endured this abuse, aborting their child can result in additional trauma that is similar to what they experienced with the rape.

Furthermore, they are subject to all the typical post-abortion symptoms. As an outsider, it's easy to look in on this situation and say, "Why should the baby pay for the sins of the father?" or "Ending the child's life doesn't take away the pain of the rape." Those statements are true, but the women in the middle of that experience are hurting and just want it all to be over. They've also been told by society, even many pro-lifers, that *this* set of circumstances makes abortion acceptable. That line of thinking couldn't be further from the truth, but it adds to the confusion.

Additionally, many women, whether they are happy about the pregnancy or not, are pressured into abortion. I've met several women who would have kept their babies if they had not been encouraged to get an abortion by people they trusted. These women are told that a baby would ruin their life, they aren't ready to be a mother, they can't afford to take a care of a child, they'll be left alone to deal with a baby, or that they'll be kicked out of the home if they choose to keep their child, among other things. This pressure to terminate a pregnancy comes from loved ones, spouses, parents, friends, co-workers, mentors, teachers, and others. Pressure of this type can come from a place of love and concern but can also often come from a place of manipulation and control.

On the other side of this coin, are the apathetic friends, family, and acquaintances who say things like, "I'll support whatever choice you make." I can't even count how many women have expressed disappointment in the people who should have displayed love and support during a difficult time. So many say they would have kept their babies if they had been encouraged by even one person to keep their baby. These women feel alone to make the decision and therefore assume they would be alone throughout the pregnancy and with raising a child.

All these situations must be handled with care because they are all accompanied by so many emotions and valid concerns. Therefore, we must be sensitive. We must love these women and families *first*, regardless of what their story is. We must also remind ourselves that there is a good chance we don't know what their full story is or what the extent of their challenges are.

As we talk with abortion-vulnerable women or those that have experienced abortion, we also need to consider what they may have been told, taught, observed, and over-heard over the years. Humans are often unable to see things clearly because what we are taught and experience greatly impacts our perspectives.

Somehow, our society has concluded that ending the life of an innocent child is a reproductive right that all women should have access to. The abortion industry has become the hero in this argument. I believe this is, in part, because abortion providers and pro-choice supporters appear to value the woman and offer opportunities for a better life. They purposefully depict pro-life advocates as radicals that solely care for the baby, not about the mother. Those fighting for abortion seem to have mistakenly determined that abortion equals freedom. But we know, all too often, freedom, according to the world, is a cover up for evil.

Many women who have experienced abortion feel as if they were deceived or tricked by the abortion industry but at the time of their abortions, those influencing their decision seemed to truly care.

The abortion industry prides itself with non-judgmental care that allows a woman to make the best personal choice. Sadly, it appears there is little focus on the other options available to a woman. In fact, the abortion industry discourages women from reversing the abortion pill, if a woman changes her mind. If pro-choice advocates were really about choice, they would support the woman's right to choose life before or after the pill is taken.

Being all about choice sounds much better than being all about the killing of babies, but the bottom line is, Pro-choice equals Pro-abortion.

The perception that the pro-choice stance is really about choice is false. Once a woman enters an abortion facility, it is more likely that she will follow through with the abortion. She enters with the idea that this is one of her choices but leaves believing there is no other option. We must be aware of this type of narrative.

It is also vital for us to remember that choosing life isn't always the easy choice. As outsiders it seems like an easy decision, right? We think, "Just keep your baby, you'll be glad you did" or "There are so many people praying for a child, just give it up for adoption."

We must not forget that all the options available to a woman facing an unplanned pregnancy are difficult. Pregnancy is extremely tough for some women, adoption is very hard emotionally, and mothering is burdensome and changes everything. Our responses need to reflect our awareness that none of this is simple. Acting callous and assuming the choice should be, "no big deal," will only erect a wall between us and the women we hope to help.

Much of our society views abortion as a superior choice to adoption. This is another sad reality that plagues our generation. Adoption isn't perfect and there have been difficult stories over the years but allowing a baby to live, while blessing a family with a child, far surpasses the choice to terminate a pregnancy. As pro-life advocates, it's time for us to reclaim and reframe adoption as the heroic choice. We need to openly discuss this option, all the time, so that a woman realizes prior to finding out she's pregnant, that adoption can be a beautiful gift for her child, for another family, and for herself. Many don't realize that through open adoption, a birthmother can choose the family she places her child with. She can also be a part of the baby's life and choose the level of interaction she'll have with her child. The idea of adoption has become so skewed and tainted but it really is the picture of love.

With all that our culture says about pregnancy and abortion, and the little value placed on human life these days, it's really no wonder that someone facing a crisis pregnancy would quickly consider it their right to choose whether they continue with the pregnancy or not. There are also countless scenarios women find themselves in which may cause abortion to seem like the best option. There are, however, some women who simply choose abortion, often repeatedly, out of convenience. Abortion is sometimes used as birth-control, as well.

Regardless of the reasons behind the choice to terminate a pregnancy, it is the killing of an innocent, voiceless, human life. This is an issue we must continue to fight against. Things may have been done poorly in the past, but it is our responsibility to move forward, and make a difference. It's time for us to Lead with Love.

But how?

How do we change the negative impact the pro-life movement has had on the fight for life? How do we navigate this sensitive topic? How do we reach women before they feel the need to make this choice? How do we fight against this evil but remain filled with love? How do we love those who seem unlovable? How do we help others see the severity of their sin? How do we put an end to this atrocity?

These are loaded questions, but one thing is for sure—*He* is the answer.

A Heart Like God's

A common misconception when someone feels drawn to God is that they must first clean themselves up and rid themselves of all sin. Thankfully, our God wants us to come to Him just as we are. When we surrender to Him, He will cleanse us and begin the process of making something beautiful out of our mess.

The same is true for those who are considering abortion or who have had an abortion. We cannot demand that a person stops sinning before we love them. In our humanity, that just doesn't make sense. It doesn't work for us. We want the negative behavior to stop before we welcome others into our lives. Loving them first, doesn't come naturally to us.

Having a heart like God will help us to lead with love.

If we have a heart like God's we will not be harsh, hateful, judgmental, critical, unforgiving, or disrespectful. We will not look down on others or talk poorly about them. With a heart like God's, we will show the world that forgiveness, love, and joy naturally occur when we consistently and authentically represent Jesus. With a heart like God's, we will live, look, and act differently than the world, which means we will also treat others differently than the world treats them.

It seems impossible for man to have a heart like God's but the Bible calls David a man after God's own heart in Acts 13:22 (NIV). David was an adulterer and a murderer, among other things. He was not perfect or pure.

So, if this is a characteristic David possessed, it is possible for each and every one of us.

To become more like the Father, we must connect with Him and allow the Holy Spirit to be at work within us. Drawing near to God through prayer, time in the Word, worship, and fellowship with other believers will teach us about God's heart and allow us to experience His love personally. Walking daily with our Creator, getting to know Him intimately, and allowing Him to guide us throughout our lives, will develop a heart like His within us.

So, what does "doing life" with God look like?

According to Ephesians 1:12 (NKJV), "We who first trusted in Christ should be to the praise of His glory." We should just *be* that way. Everything we are, everything we say, and everything we do should be to the praise of His glory. Living out life with a heart like God's means we will just exist to praise His name! That doesn't mean we won't mess up, that we'll never sin again, or that we're perfect. It simply means that with our lives, we desire to honor God and glorify Him. And when we do slip up and fall short, we know He is there to pick us up.

God's voice is one of hope and kindness, leading us home. Therefore, having a heart like God's means our voice will resemble His. John 15:12 (NLT) says, "This is my commandment, that you love one another as I have loved you." Therefore, having a heart like God's means we will love others the way Jesus has loved us. Psalm 107:2a (ESV) says, "Let the redeemed of the Lord say so." If we are a people after God's own heart, we will say so! Words of thanksgiving and joy will fall from our lips because we belong to Him!

> "And pray in the Spirit on all occasions with all kinds of prayers and requests. With this in mind, be alert and always keep on praying for all the Lord's people." Ephesians 6:18 (NIV)

As God's people, we will be in prayer for those we encounter. We will also pray for leaders of all kinds: pastors, ministry leaders, teachers, politicians, etc. We will pray over the roles they serve in, but also over their potential to influence a woman who may consider abortion.

It's also important for us to be aware of the importance of humility. If we are looking down on others, we cannot also be humble enough to be used by the Holy Spirit. We are simply tools in the mighty hands of the Father. Pride causes us to be unusable. Humility gives us the correct posture. God can do more than we ask or imagine when His people humble themselves!

Embrace the Battle

I'm often amazed by how flippantly the title "hero" is handed out these days. In my opinion, a hero is someone who risks their life for another person. For example, I consider firefighters heroes. These individuals run toward the fire instead of away from it.

For those fighting for life to save women and babies, we need to embrace the battle we've been chosen to fight. I believe I hear God saying, "Run toward the fire, faithful warriors!"

Here are a few helpful reminders as we run:

- How people view us is based on our behavior, not our belief system.
- We cannot look down on others and love them like Jesus at the same time.
- As Believers, we need to live a life worthy of the call on our lives.
- Being right doesn't give us permission to be unkind.
- We cannot bend people to our worldview- we must introduce them to the ONE who changed our world view.
- Actions Matter. Words Matter.
- It will be impossible to be open to the Holy Spirit's leading if we already have our speeches and condemning statements prepared.
- We should focus more on the beauty of God instead of how terrible hell is.
- We are a part of God's plan for the salvation of others.
- We are God's family. We mustn't ruin how others view the church because of our actions, views, words, etc.
- In order to rescue someone who is drowning, we need to jump into the water, where they are. Yelling from the bridge doesn't help.
- Our influence can shift the tide.

Abortion is the *opposite* of the gospel. It says, "You must die so I can live." As Christ-followers we are called to live out the gospel, which says to an abortion-vulnerable woman and those who have chosen abortion in the past, "Jesus died, so you can live."

4

It's All about Choices

THROUGHOUT THE PROCESS OF writing this book, I've become increasingly aware that the fight against abortion involves a plethora of choices. Of course, our minds go directly to the "My body; my choice" mantra, but it's so much more than that. From the choice to engage in sexual activity to the choice to speak up about this issue, there are countless ways choices impact the fight for life. These include choices made by individuals having abortions, abortion workers, pro-choice and pro-life advocates, churches, families, and even our nation.

Our Nation and its Choices

> "The Lord said to Moses, "Say to the Israelites: 'Any Israelite or any foreigner residing in Israel who sacrifices any of his children to Molech is to be put to death. The members of the community are to stone him. I will set my face against him and will cut him off from his people; for by sacrificing his children to Molech, he has defiled my sanctuary and profaned my holy name. If the members of the community close their eyes when that man sacrifices one of his children to Molech and if they fail to put him to death, I will set my face against him and his family and will cut them off from their people together with all who follow him in prostituting themselves to Molech." (Leviticus 20:1–5 (NIV)

These verses are a portion of the instructions from God, the Israelites received at the base of Mount Sinai. These laws were a guide for the Israelites, so they might maintain a right relationship with God, live set apart, and deal with sin and its destructive consequences.

Molech was a dreadful idol worshipped through child sacrifice. It's believed that in worship of Molech, a statue representing him was heated until it was red hot and then living infants were placed into the hands of the statue.

As revealed in these verses, God is absolutely opposed to this type of sacrifice. Not only would the idol worshipper be put to death, but anyone else in the community who "closed their eyes" to the act would be cut off from their people and God would turn His face from them.

How does this apply to our nation, in our time? Although it's a difficult concept, it's not hard to correlate child sacrifice and abortion. We have elevated ourselves as the idol for numerous reasons, therefore making it permissible to sacrifice our children on the altar of self.

Many also believe aborted fetuses are currently sold for research purposes and/or rituals. If God hated child sacrifice in the Old Testament, He still does.

Just as noted in Leviticus chapter 20, not only will God set His face against those who abort their children, He will also turn His face against those who sit back and do nothing about it.

Thankfully, because of Jesus, we can be reconciled with God, even when we've broken His heart and disobeyed His laws, if we cry out to Him, repent of our ways, and surrender our lives to Him.

> "For if, while we were God's enemies, we were reconciled to him through the death of his Son, how much more, having been reconciled, shall we be saved through his life!" Romans 5:10 (NIV)

God's willingness to forgive us, however, does not give us a license to continue with our destructive choices or to pretend we are unaware of what's happening all around us. Make no mistake about it, God holds us, as a nation, accountable for abortion.

According to Wikipedia, 70 percent of Americans identify as Christian. [1]It seems that many Bible-believing, Christ-following Americans would have a bigger impact on the state of our country and the fight against abortion. As Christians, we cannot continue going to church on Sunday and voting for abortion on Tuesday.

We also cannot go on turning a blind eye on this topic. Choosing not to pay attention to an issue is still making a choice. We can say, "I just don't

---

1. "Christians in the USA." 1.

want to get involved," but when we make that choice, we are silently aiding the abortion industry.

There is a common argument that claims making abortion illegal will force women to seek "back-alley abortions." This argument attempts to redirect the focus of the issue, implying making abortion legal keeps women safe.

> *As Christians, we cannot continue going to church on Sunday and voting for abortion on Tuesday.*

According to Dr. Kathi Aultman, former abortionist and Medical Director for Planned Parenthood, "*In 1972, the year before Roe v Wade, thirty-nine women died from illegal abortion, and twenty-four women died from legal abortion. In 1973, the year of Roe v Wade, nineteen women died from illegal abortion, and twenty-five women died from legal abortion. So, in the year that abortion was nationally legalized, more women died from legal abortion than illegal abortion.*" [2]

No matter what, abortion isn't safe. Whether women choose to have legal abortions or illegal ones, women are harmed by this procedure. Either way, it's a decision they are making; a personal decision that is between them and God.

The possibility that a woman may have an illegal abortion is not reason enough for an entire country to make abortion legal. Allowing abortion to be freely available and legal in our country makes it an issue between the entire nation and God.

As a nation made up of so many professing Christians, we need to take a stand. We must no longer choose to be held accountable for the decisions that some make or close our eyes to the tragedy happening all around us.

The Pro-Life Movement and our Choices

Everyone involved in the pro-life movement has already made a choice. We've chosen to stand up for those who cannot stand up for themselves. There are many subsequent choices that need to be made by pro-life

2. "Back Alley Abortions". 10

advocates, however. Each day we choose how we will act, what we say, the attitude we will portray, and how we will treat others.

This reminds me of the story of the Good Samaritan. In this parable, a man asks Jesus what he must do to inherit eternal life. "Jesus answered, "'Love the Lord your God with all your heart and with all your soul and with all your strength and with all your mind;' and 'Love your neighbor as yourself.'" (Luke 10:27 NIV) The man then asks, "Who is my neighbor?"

> "In reply Jesus said: "A man was going down from Jerusalem to Jericho, when he was attacked by robbers. They stripped him of his clothes, beat him and went away, leaving him half dead. A priest happened to be going down the same road, and when he saw the man, he passed by on the other side. So too, a Levite, when he came to the place and saw him, passed by on the other side. But a Samaritan, as he traveled, came where the man was; and when he saw him, he took pity on him. He went to him and bandaged his wounds, pouring on oil and wine. Then he put the man on his own donkey, brought him to an inn and took care of him. The next day he took out two denarii and gave them to the innkeeper. 'Look after him,' he said, 'and when I return, I will reimburse you for any extra expense you may have. "Which of these three do you think was a neighbor to the man who fell into the hands of robbers?" The expert in the law replied, "The one who had mercy on him." Jesus told him, "Go and do likewise." Luke 10:30-37 (NIV)

In this story, the Samaritan was the most unlikely person to stop and help the injured man. Those listening to Jesus as He shared this parable would have recognized that fact right away. After all, it was no secret that Jews and Samaritans were enemies. They would have been even more shocked by the Samaritan's subsequent choices. He not only checked on the injured man but also cared for his wounds, carried him on his donkey, and paid for his room and board at an inn. The Samaritan didn't just do the bare minimum. He went above and beyond for someone society said he was supposed to hate.

How many times do we choose to follow in the Good Samaritan's footsteps?

As pro-life advocates, we are given the opportunity to make this choice repeatedly. When we encounter someone considering abortion, we get to choose how we will speak to her. When we are discussing abortion with others, we get to choose whether our words will bring life or death. When we meet someone who has experienced abortion, we get to decide if we will condemn them or show them God's love and mercy.

We will never know how great the impact of our choices may be in the fight for life, but we can be sure, choosing to be more like the Good Samaritan will always be what God desires of us.

This is God's issue. He is Pro-Life. We must choose to represent Him well.

The Choices of Others

As much as we'd like to, we are unable to make choices for other people. We can try to influence them but ultimately, everyone makes their own decisions. While the choices others make can often seem absurd or even infuriate us, it's important for us to be aware of the choices they face.

In connection with the abortion issue, there are many choices being made daily. Here are a few for us to consider:

- Should I engage in sexual activity?
- Should I have protected or unprotected sex?
- Should I take a pregnancy test?
- Should I keep my baby?
- Should I choose adoption?
- Should I tell my family about my pregnancy?
- Should I go to the local Pregnancy Resource Center?
- Should I seek help from my church family?
- Should I tell the father about this baby?
- Should I talk to someone who has had an abortion?
- Should I believe what the pro-life people are saying?
- Should I attend those parenting classes and accept that assistance?
- Should I believe I can be a good mother?
- Should I trust that God has a plan for me and this baby?
- Should I talk about what I've done or just keep it hidden?
- Should I believe that God can forgive me?
- Should I just give up?

These choices are real. These choices are heavy. These choices are important.

The abortion industry says they are all about choice but, if a woman chooses to go to the clinic, she will likely believe the lies she's told and end up believing she has no choice at all. That's why, as those fighting for life, we must remember the power of her choice! Whether it's outside of the abortion facility or sitting in a youth group, a woman can choose whether she wants to, or will ever want to, end the life of her child.

Our time with people is so brief in the grand scheme of things. We quickly have a negative or positive impact on the lives of others. We must choose to make those moments count. So, whether in the middle of a crisis, or simply in the process of forming her opinion, we should always be helping women choose to believe in themselves and the beauty of life. For those who have made a choice they regret, we can choose to be the ones who point her to a God who loves her, forgives her, and restores her.

Our Choices

We've talked about the choices of our nation, choices of the pro-life movement, and the choices of others so, it's only fair that we also closely consider the choices we make personally.

Although some may disagree, humans were not created for the purpose of being comfortable and happy. God created us to reflect Jesus and be difference makers. Often, making a difference in this world will take us far out of our comfort zones. If we're unwilling to go there with God, so we can maintain our happiness and comfort; we will end up missing out.

> One of the purest and most undefiled demonstrations of the gospel is to see the hard places and broken people and move toward them, not away. This will not happen in our comfort zones and we will not be accepted by others unless we are humble and kind.

God blesses those who are willing to be used by Him. While it may feel like a blessing to remain in the little safety bubble we've created for ourselves, God has so much more in store for us.

"I have come that they may have life and have it abundantly." John 10:10b (ESV)

One of the purest and most undefiled demonstrations of the gospel is to see hard places and broken people and move toward them, not away. This will not happen in our comfort zones and will not be accepted by others, unless we are humble and kind.

The post-abortive and abortion-vulnerable are broken people in very difficult places. They need us but we must choose to move toward them.

We must also choose to be intentional with our words and our attitudes because those we could impact the most are listening. When we are callous and speak with anger instead of grace, they will choose to hide for fear of judgement or shame.

Authenticity is another important choice we have to make. It feels easier to hide our difficulties and pretend we never struggle, but when we choose to be authentic, it opens the door for connections to be made and relationships to be born. It's important to remember that when we don't share the tests we've endured, we devalue the testimony we've been given.

When we say, "I'll bring my brokenness so you can bring yours," we are humbling ourselves and allowing others to believe we value them enough to be genuine with them. They will not fear our judgement. Plus, it's much easier to be open with someone who says, "I've been there," or "I struggle too," than it is to talk with those who come across as perfect and problem-free.

To make the most impact, we need to realize how easy it can be to act like a Pharisee. The Pharisees were the highly educated, religious men during Jesus' time on earth. They said all the right things and they knew all the laws, but they missed the point entirely. We can choose to say the right things while pretending we have no faults, or we can choose to love like Jesus.

Jesus was authentic and He always chose to love first.

Choices are Important to God

God created choice and He deemed it important enough to give us freewill. He wants us to have input in our lives and in the lives of others. He wants us to choose to follow Him and live for Him. Ultimately, even salvation and eternal life are all about choice.

As advocates for life, choices are something we should not take lightly. Some decisions are insignificant and easily forgotten while others are a matter of life and death. Moving forward, it's my prayer that we would consider the impact of our choices as a nation and as individuals. May we also be aware of the choices others are making and the impact our choices have in the fight against abortion.

5

Understanding the Abortion-Vulnerable Woman

Who are Abortion-Vulnerable Women?

MANY PEOPLE TEND TO have a distorted idea of women who have abortions. Most believe women seeking abortions are of a specific ethnicity, age group, or socioeconomic class. This line of thinking could not be further from the truth. In this chapter, we will discuss who the abortion-vulnerable woman is, her reasons for choosing abortion, why adoption isn't appealing to her, what she experiences, and the view we should have of her. It's my prayer that these women will come alive to everyone who reads this book. Women considering abortion are not just in big cities or on college campuses. The ladies who will choose or have already chosen abortion are all around us. We know this is true because one in four women have had an abortion. They are in our neighborhoods, families, schools, offices, and yes, even in our churches.

According to a 2014 survey published by theconversation.com involving over 8,000 women who had abortions, it's more common for white women to have abortions than Black or Hispanic women. 40 percent of women having abortions have attended college and 23 percent are college graduates. The most common age range for abortions is twenty to twenty-four years old. Nine percent are performed on women between thirty-five to thirty-nine years old. Thirty-three percent of women having abortions already have two or more children. [1]

As I've talked with people and groups all over the country about this topic, it's been clear that most assume teenage pregnancies make up the majority of abortions. That isn't true. Teenage girls make up less than 12 percent of all abortions.

It's also important for us to acknowledge a 2015 study by Care Net, which found that 70 percent of women who have had abortions indicate they are Christians. One-third of those women said they attend church once a week or more. The study also shows that *only* 38 percent of women who have had abortions agree that churches are a safe place to talk about their unplanned pregnancy.[2] It's heartbreaking to realize that so many church-attending ladies, who discover an unwanted pregnancy, run to the abortion clinic instead of to their church family. This is another reason why *Lead with Love* is necessary, for the pro-life movement and the church alike.

These statistics may come as a surprise to some. Typically, people who are unfamiliar with this issue believe that the only women getting abortions are poor, young, uneducated, Black or Hispanic women, who have no religious background. That assumption is false. Women of all ages, ethnicities, backgrounds, education levels, and church experience choose to have abortions.

There is also a misconception about abortion-vulnerable women being victims of rape or having exceptionally bad health concerns. Even some people who identify as pro-life believe that abortion should only be allowed in the cases of rape, incest, or for medical reasons. In my opinion, this argument is often used as a buffer, to keep from having to fully take a stance against abortion. If we believe life begins at conception and that abortion ends a life, isn't that still true in the case of rape, incest, or medical conditions? For someone to say they are pro-life, except in those cases, causes a major break in their stance that all life is valuable.

The truth is, according to Abort73.org, of all the women having abortions, less than 1 percent are victims of rape and/or incest. Less than 7 percent are experiencing fetal or maternal health problems. That means, more than 92 percent of abortions are not *at all* related to rape, incest, or medical issues.[3]

1. Ireland, "Who Chooses Abortion." 10.

2. "Abortion in Church." 6, 20, 32.

3. "Abortion Statistics." 25.

So why do so many people hang their hats on the argument that abortion is okay in those cases? I believe it's because it is simply easier to take that stance. It sounds compassionate and loving toward those who are experiencing a difficult situation. It's important to understand, however, that many rape victims, who have gotten pregnant and subsequently had an abortion, feel as if they were being victimized again. The ability to end the life of the child conceived in rape did not help these victims, it only made the situation worse and more painful.

Serena Dyksen, author of *She Found His Grace*, says, *"I think people need to understand that abortion did not undo my rape. It doesn't take that pain away but only adds more pain. We can't help what others do to us but it's a heavy weight knowing we ended a life. I know for me; I would never end a life on purpose. That's not in my DNA, so abortion after rape was devastating. Not to mention, it felt like I was being raped all over again."*

Those who have abortions due to medical reasons often spend the rest of their lives wondering if the doctors were right or wrong. They wish they had allowed the scenario to play out because at least that way, they wouldn't have been the one to end the baby's life. They also often suffer emotionally after abortion.

In his article, *Aborting the Wanted Child*, Paul Sullins states, *"I recently found that the risk of depression, suicidality, or anxiety disorders from such abortions [of wanted babies] was almost four times higher than for women who had aborted a child in an unwanted pregnancy."* [4]

Victims of rape and/or incest and those dealing with medical issues only make up a tiny fraction of the women choosing abortion. Even in those cases, most regret the choice.

It's been said that half of women having abortions have had one previously. So, not only are there women all around us who have had abortions, many have experienced abortion multiple times.

Regardless of race, age, religious affiliation, socioeconomic status, or any other characteristic, all women considering abortion are children of God. They are valuable and loved because He says so.

> "Rich and poor have this in common: The LORD is the Maker of them all." Proverbs 22:2 (NIV)

> "I have loved you with an everlasting love; therefore, I have continued my faithfulness to you." Jeremiah 31:3 (ESV)

---

4. Sullins, "Aborting the Wanted Child." 1.

"For God so loved the world, He gave His only Son, that whoever believes in Him should not perish but have eternal life." John 3:16 (ESV)

"God shows his love for us in that while we were still sinners, Christ died for us." Romans 5:8 (ESV)

Knowing who abortion-vulnerable women are is vital in the fight against abortion because our stereotypical mindsets about the topic are an obstacle that could easily be removed. Realizing that crisis pregnancies are something people from all walks of life encounter, will help us relate to those considering abortion and allow them to feel less judgement from pro-life individuals and organizations.

Why Would She Choose Abortion?

It's easy to think about abortion and simply say, "How could anyone ever do that?"

> *Knowing who abortion-vulnerable women are is vital in the fight against abortion because our stereotypical mindsets about the topic are an obstacle that could easily be removed.*

For those who have never faced an unplanned pregnancy, it can be difficult to imagine considering the choice to abort. For those who know the truth about abortion, or for those who chose life when faced with a crisis pregnancy, it's hard to imagine being naïve to the tragedy. Therefore, I want to expound on the reasons why many women are vulnerable to abortion. Of course, every individual and situation are unique, but it's important for us to understand why women often choose this so-called, "easy way out."

An unplanned pregnancy is a crisis for many, especially those who are unmarried, are unemployed, have an abusive partner, or have health concerns, among many other things. Discovering that she is pregnant is often stressful emotionally and physically for a woman. On top of the usual hormones, emotional difficulties, and physical symptoms associated with pregnancy, these women are bombarded with questions, fears, concerns, doubts, and often, pressure from others. This news also blind-sides many women, causing them to feel rushed to figure out a solution to this "problem."

Consider a time when you were given shocking news that you weren't prepared for. Do you recall how desperate you felt as you tried to figure out how to get beyond the crisis? The same is true for a woman who is stunned by the news that she is pregnant. She often feels hopeless and alone, some-times she already cares for other children or family members, and many times she believes this child is the worst thing that could happen to her.

While balancing all the usual conditions of her life, she is suddenly faced with a monumental decision. A decision that is difficult to talk about with anyone, feels shameful, and is overwhelming. The abortion industry claims to be "non-judgmental" and offers "Care no matter what," so it's no wonder women would consider the clinic a reliable resource. There are also many cases when a woman believes she must hide her pregnancy therefore, abortion seems like the only option.

Women seek abortions for a variety of reasons. In most cases, they give multiple explanations for their choice to abort. According to a study by BMC Women's Health, "40 percent of women say finances were their main reason for choosing abortion, 36 percent say it just wasn't the right time for a baby, 29 percent needed to focus on the children they already had, and 20 percent were concerned that a baby would interfere with future opportunities.[5]

Issues with the father of the child play a role in the decision to abort 31 percent of the time. These reasons include not being married, low in-come, and the partner not wanting a child. 7 percent of women did not feel emotionally or mentally prepared to be a parent. 4 percent simply did not want to have a baby. There is also a mindset that occurred 12 percent of the time, involving the woman wanting a better life for the baby than she could provide. Sadly, she believed the lie that ending the child's life would be better than the life she could give it. [6]

Even if she is unsure of what to do, once a woman visits an abortion clinic, even if it's just for information about this option, she is typically per-suaded to go along with the procedure. The fact is the abortion workers are skilled at doing so. They understand the psychology of it and play on the woman's vulnerabilities.

---

5. BMC Women's Health, "Understanding Why." Table 2.
6. BMC Women's Health, "Understanding Why." Table 2.

In an article I wrote for Live Action News, I shared Kara's abortion story. Upon arrival, the employee she counseled with, told her an abortion was a good choice because it would allow her to still attend college and someday have a family—when she was prepared for it. Kara explained, *"She said she could see that I wasn't ready yet and was 'proud of me' for making such a 'selfless decision.'"* [7]

Determining that abortion is a selfless act is not uncommon. Women choosing abortion often believe they are making a sacrifice to preserve their own lives or the lives of others in their family. They see it as something they must do because of the situation they are in. It may be because many women experience a fight-or-flight response when faced with the news of an unplanned pregnancy. This is an automatic physiological reaction that occurs when someone is confronted with something terrifying; it's also known as the acute stress response. When this happens, women find themselves in survival mode and are not thinking clearly.

It's also important to be aware of all the lies modern day females hear in the world today. Women are inundated with media-driven ideas like, "I'm only valuable if I have a boy-friend or husband," "Sex outside of marriage is normal and has no consequences," "I should do whatever makes me happy," "God just wants us to be happy," "A baby would ruin my life and prevent me from reaching my goals," "I have the right to choose whatever I think is best," "Abortion is an empowering choice," and "I must appear perfect and hide my emotions."

Much of what they are told about abortion is demeaning toward women and causes them to doubt their ability to be a mother and fulfill their dreams. Women were designed by God to be mothers. It's not empowering for a woman to kill her children.

On top of the lies they've heard; most women are terribly naïve or misinformed about life in the womb and abortion. In public schools today, abortion is simply listed as an option when a woman discovers she's pregnant. The details of the procedure are not shared, and the lasting impact abortion has is not mentioned. It many cases, abortion is portrayed as a form of birth control. When a woman faces an unplanned pregnancy and is uninformed or misinformed about abortion, she is much more likely to view it as a valid option.

We mustn't look past the likelihood that many women entering the doors of an abortion clinic are also feeling an immense sense of pressure to

7. Shaw, "Pregnant Again." 5.

abort. Pressure comes in many forms including social and economic pressure, subtle or blatant pressure from friends or family, manipulation by the father of the child, and fear of abandonment. Sometimes the pressure is simply perceived, while other times, it is a reality.

Pressure to abort can also come from the baby's father if he takes a "hands-off" approach to the topic, saying that he supports what she chooses. That sounds nice but, it places the decision fully on the shoulders of the woman, leaving her feeling alone and unsupported.

Sex-trafficking should also be noted because pimps often use abortion to maximize their profits. Sex-traffickers and abortionists alike, exploit women and profit from this terrible form of human suffering. Kathy Hadel, a sex trafficking survivor says, "*Many people don't realize that abortions are quite common in the sex trafficking world. Even with protection (which isn't always used), chances of the women getting pregnant are somewhat high, considering the number of johns they must service each night. Some are forced by their pimps to abort; others realize they are not equipped to raise a child and choose to end their pregnancy. Either way, it's a decision that will haunt these women the rest of their lives. I know it does mine.*"

A study published in the Journal of American Physicians and Surgeons showed that nearly 75 percent of women experience, "*at least subtle forms of pressure to terminate their pregnancies.*" The study also revealed that out of the 987 women surveyed, nearly 60 percent decided to abort "to make others happy" and almost 30 percent were "afraid that they would lose their partner" if they didn't abort their pregnancies. [8]

The same study also showed that two thirds of the women knew in their hearts that abortion was wrong, and more than 67 percent said it was one of the hardest decisions of their lives. [9]

I believe these studies expose the truth about who is choosing abortion in America. When pressure and manipulation are introduced into the equation, a woman no longer has the right to freely choose. In these cases, women who are supposedly choosing to kill their babies are succumbing to the pressure placed on them by others.

So, why would a woman even consider abortion? The reasons are numerous, but most are based on a foundation of lies and/or a lack of true information. These ladies are facing a crisis, feel alone, are being pressured, and aren't thinking clearly. In many cases, these women are victims because

8. Coleman, Ph.D., "Women Who Suffered." 3.
9. Coleman, Ph.D., "Women Who Suffered." 3.

they are persuaded to make this choice during a time of desperation and fear. Most aren't happy about their choice but felt there was no other option.

Why Doesn't She Just Choose Adoption?

Adoption is a beautiful thing. The Bible mentions it multiple times and even contains an adoption story in the Old Testament. In Exodus chapter 2, Moses' mother placed him in a basket in the river to save him from the Pharaoh's decree that all Hebrew baby boys must be killed. One of the Pharaoh's daughters found Moses and adopted him into her family.

It's clear that adoption is close to God's heart because He also chose to model it for us by adopting us through His Son, Jesus.

> "He predestined us for adoption as sons through Jesus Christ, according to the purpose of his will." Ephesians 1:5 (ESV)

> "But to all who did receive him, who believed in his name, he gave the right to become children of God." John 1:12 (ESV)

Adoption is a wonderful alternative to abortion but sadly, it isn't viewed that way. There is a belief that because our adoption system is overwhelmed and has many flaws, abortion is a better alternative. Adoption is also considered to be a traumatic option for the birth mother and the child.

While there is some truth in those beliefs, my heart breaks for those who think it would be better to end a child's life than choose adoption, simply because the system is flawed and there is potential for trauma. Even those born into a wonderful, loving home could endure trauma, and many aspects of life in general are flawed. These simply are not valid reasons to abort a baby.

It is estimated that there are more than 600,000 abortions each year, while there are less than 15,000 adoptions. Misconceptions about adoption play a factor in that harsh reality. Many women believe that abortion is less expensive than placing a child up for adoption, that abortion will have less emotional side effects, and that choosing adoption means they'll be placing their baby into a nightmare situation.

The truth is, adoption is completely free for birth mothers and in some cases, assistance for living expenses and medical needs are provided. Most women who choose adoption are more satisfied with their decision than those who chose abortion because they know they gave their child a chance at life.

Yes, there are terrible adoption stories, but there are also incredible adoption stories. Adoption has changed a lot over the years. The process is also very different than portrayed in the media. Now, the process places the control in the hands of the birth mother, allowing her to choose which type of adoption she prefers.

With open adoption, the birth mother is able to choose the child's parents, choose whether to be involved in the child's life, and have regular visits with the child, if desired.

I also believe abortion is often chosen over adoption because women were created with a motherly instinct, whether they want to be mothers or not. This instinct causes some women to view adoption in an interesting way. They see it as the death of their role as a mother and the death of their relationship with their child through abandonment. Their motherly instinct tells them that they will wonder about their baby for the rest of their life, which leads them to believe abortion is a better choice.

Adoption is absolutely a better alternative to abortion, but it's also a decision that isn't as easy as it seems. There are many complex thoughts and emotions which make it difficult for a woman to "just choose adoption."

How Does She Feel?

When my oldest son was about three years old, he decided to use his artistic skills to decorate the wall in our living room. Afterward, he tried to hide what he had done by wiping the crayon with a baby wipe, but his attempts were unsuccessful. When my husband and I discovered the scribbles and questioned him about it, he blamed it on his brother, who was an infant. He must have thought we would believe that our baby wrote on the walls even though he couldn't sit up or hold a crayon.

He felt terrible and was ashamed of himself. His attempt to blame-shift was out of desperation. He wasn't thinking clearly when he chose his baby brother as his scapegoat. When we sat him down and talked with him lovingly, he finally admitted to the offense and helped me scrub the wall. When the artwork had been erased, he hugged me and thanked me for helping him. He never drew on the walls or furniture again.

I believe many women confronted with an unplanned pregnancy can relate to the way my son felt. They've made a choice which led to this seemingly horrible outcome. They try to hide it and are desperate to make it go away, often based on illogical thinking. In many cases, if someone lovingly offers help and support, their fear dissipates, and they begin to see clearly.

I wonder what would have happened if we had yelled at my little artist, shaming him, and calling him a liar. Would he have admitted what he had done? Would he have hugged me and thanked me for helping him clean it up? Would he ever feel comfortable talking to us when he makes a mistake in the future?

It's something to consider when talking to or about abortion-vulnerable women. Their shame, fear, desperation, and illogical thinking will keep them from sharing their unwanted news with others, especially with those who have openly spoken with disdain about this topic. If they decide to be open with someone, the way they are treated will greatly impact their decisions and their willingness to expose their mistakes and failures in the future.

When women unexpectedly find out they are carrying a baby, they are often shocked, begin operating in crisis-mode, and have tunnel vision. Many feel conflicted because abortion is a legal option, and the world says it's the easy way out. But deep down, most know abortion is wrong.

When I found out I was pregnant at sixteen, I couldn't believe it at first but quickly assumed my life was coming to end. When my pediatrician offered to make an abortion appointment for me, it appeared to be the only light at the end of a very dark, long tunnel. I knew what the word abortion meant but had no idea what it entailed. I had never heard anyone admit to having one, but I knew it was legal.

The doctor who made the appointment for me was very pregnant herself. I remember saying to her, "You must hate me. You're having to make an abortion appointment for me when you're so pregnant." She replied, "If I were only sixteen, I would do the same thing." My mom was in the exam room with us and seemed to be okay with the option as well. With all of my emotions, the doctor's advice, my mom's silent approval, my boyfriend's "hands-off" support, and the fact that abortion was legal, I chose to abort my baby.

Somewhere, deep inside, I knew it wasn't the right choice, but I actively chose not to think about it being wrong because I was afraid I might talk myself out of it. I believed abortion was something I just had to do. I felt an intense urgency to get it taken care of so I could pretend it had never happened.

Less than twenty-four hours after hearing the news that I was pregnant, I had a vacuum aspiration abortion. When I walked out of the clinic,

I was no longer the same girl. I wore a shroud of shame and immediately began working very hard to hide my experience and numb my pain.

Sometimes I wonder what would have happened if even one person had talked with me about other options or encouraged me to keep my baby. My husband, who is also the boy that got me pregnant at sixteen, believes I would have chosen life if he had only suggested it and shown me support. I think he's right.

An abortion-vulnerable woman is exactly that, vulnerable. I wonder how many women would choose life if they simply felt loved, supported, and heard. How many women would change their minds if someone gently shared the truth about abortion with them and called out the strength within them? If these women are vulnerable enough to be talked into abortion, they are likely vulnerable enough to be talked out of it.

> *An abortion-vulnerable woman is exactly that, vulnerable.*
> *If they are vulnerable enough to be talked into an abortion, they are likely vulnerable enough to be talked out of it.*

My oldest son, the artist I mentioned previously, is now thirteen and loves history. One day, as we served as sidewalk advocates together outside of our local abortion clinic, he compared the scenario to the Boxer Rebellion. I had no idea what he was referring to but as he explained, I could definitely see the connection.

The Boxer Rebellion occurred in northern China between 1899 and 1901. This peasant uprising aimed to eliminate foreign influences. Among other things, foreign trade and Christian missionaries were causes for the rebellion. The Opium War forced China to open itself up to foreign trade and resentment built up as more and more missionaries entered the area. The revolt was an attempt to get rid of all foreign religions, cultures, and influences.

My son explained that Great Britain and other countries simply wanted to trade with China and the missionaries just wanted to share the Good News with them. China didn't see it that way. They saw them as invaders and revolted because of this belief.

Then my son compared the women entering the clinic to the Chinese. He also compared the sidewalk advocates to the foreign trade and missionaries. He said, "We just want to help these ladies, but they don't see it that way. They view us as foreign influences. They put their guard up and avoid us because they see us as invaders of their privacy."

His observation is true. Regardless of our intentions, abortion-vulnerable women most likely view pro-life advocates and our opinions as foreign influences. Therefore, our demeanor and attitude are so very important. Yelling, shaming, holding graphic signs, and pointing fingers will never draw someone to us, especially when they already view us as invaders. If we want women to give us the opportunity to offer them help and hope, we must have an inviting presence that encourages them to believe that we are not foreign influences and that we can be trusted.

This also proves why the voice of post-abortive women is valuable and necessary. When an abortion-vulnerable woman hears someone say, "I've been in your shoes and chose abortion," they quickly realize this person is not an invader. They will lay their guard down and willingly invite her in.

Abortion-vulnerable women are facing a difficult decision. While some may flippantly abort their babies, most struggle with the decision, many are pressured, and almost all regret it tremendously. No matter what, abortion isn't the easy option it's portrayed to be.

How Should We View Her?

It's easy to look at others and point out their faults. It's also easy to assume that we are superior and would never make the same mistakes. When thinking about abortion-vulnerable women, I believe we must put away our assumptions, refuse to be judgmental, and remember that we, too, are sinners.

Consider a couple involved in an extra-marital affair. The only difference between the woman who discovers an unwanted pregnancy and the man who got her pregnant, is that her secret sin is exposed as her belly grows. We shouldn't view her as more of a sinner than her boyfriend is, should we? They both chose to have sex outside of marriage, but she must carry around the consequence.

The same is true with the sin of abortion. Yes, it is murder. Yes, it is a sin. But according to God, no sin is weightier than another. In His eyes, we are all sinners, equally.

> "For whoever keeps the whole law and yet stumbles at just one point is guilty of breaking all of it." James 2:10 (NIV)

> "As it is written: 'None is righteous, not one.'" Romans 3:10 (NIV)

Therefore, we must not look at an abortion-vulnerable woman and only see her as someone about to commit a terrible sin. We should view her as someone who is vulnerable, hurting, scared, and in need of support and love. We should refuse to assume that we would make a better choice because we have no idea how complex her situation is or the amount of pressure she is dealing with. We should be aware of our own tendency to mess up and our own great need of a Savior.

Jesus gives a wonderful example of how we should view and treat those we know are sinning. In John chapter 4, Jesus sat down by a well in Samaria. When a Samaritan woman joined Him at the well to collect water, Jesus asked her for a drink. She pointed out that she was a Samaritan, and He was a Jew therefore, He shouldn't be associating with her. Jesus explained that if she knew who He was, she would be asking Him for water—- Living Water. She immediately wanted the water that would cause her to never thirst again. Jesus instructed her to get her husband and she replied, saying she wasn't married. Jesus knew that she had been married five times and was currently living with a man who wasn't her husband. He told her all the things He knew about her, and she was amazed. He also revealed that He was the Messiah she had heard about, which compelled her to run back to town and tell everyone. She said, "He told me everything I ever did," and because of her testimony, many Samaritans believed in Him.

It's important to note that the woman was at the well during an un-usual time of day. Typically, Samaritan women gathered water early in the day to avoid the heat, but we know she was at the well much later in the day because John 4:6 (NIV) says it was about noon. Theologians believe the woman was most likely a social outcast because she was alone, gathering water at such and odd hour. The woman's marital status and her past most likely played a part in her being an outcast.

The woman quickly noticed something different about Jesus because of His friendliness towards her. This would have impressed her because it was no secret that Jews and Samaritans wanted nothing to do with one another. Not only was Jesus unexpectedly kind to the Samaritan, but He also made her aware of the life-giving water that only He can give.

Additionally, Jesus asked her to get her husband, which was cultur-ally appropriate during this time. Jesus knew she had been married mul-tiple times and currently lived with someone who wasn't her husband, but that didn't keep Him from caring for her. He knew all of this before she ever walked up to the well, yet He chose to talk kindly with her and reveal

Himself to her. I believe it's because He chose to see her, and not focus on her sin, when He looked her.

John 4:27(NIV) tells us the disciples were shocked to find Jesus talking with a Samaritan woman, which was culturally inappropriate to say the least, but no one questioned Him. They had most likely learned that Jesus didn't care much about man-made rules but instead, always had good reasons for His actions.

The Samaritan woman was impressed by Jesus' love for her which caused her to feel safe with Him even though He confronted her sinful past. His love had drawn her in, and she would forever be changed because of it. Not only her, but also many in her community.

There are many stories in the Bible that reveal the love Jesus had for sinners, but I chose to share this one because I believe it connects deeply with our topic of discussion. Abortion-vulnerable women are a lot like the Samaritan woman. They often feel alone and cast aside because of their pregnancies. They are considering a choice they believe will hide their sin or preserve their life in some way. The Samaritan woman did the same by going to the well at a different time than the other women in her village. Abortion-vulnerable women often assume everyone will be hateful and judgmental toward them and are surprised when they receive support and love instead. They are also thirsty; thirsty for all that Jesus has to offer them.

Jesus knew everything the woman had done, which probably included a lot more than just the five marriages and live-in boyfriend, but He was entirely kind and gentle. He did not withhold anything from her, but instead offered her all that she would ever need.

Jesus was also able to confront her sin, which is something many pro-life advocates feel strongly about. We are not called to condemn, but with the power of the gospel and the Holy Spirit, our loving kindness can lead others to realize the truth about their sinful nature. She felt safe with Jesus, even though He pointed out her sin. Abortion-vulnerable women can feel that same safety with us, when we lead with love, like Jesus did.

Even when we know someone is considering abortion or watch her walk into a clinic, we need to model Jesus' behavior. Remembering all that we've discussed in this chapter will enable us to view these women with love, even though we do not agree with the choice they're considering.

6

Understanding the Post-Abortive Woman

As a woman who has experienced abortion, I cannot stress enough how important it is for the pro-life community to better understand the post-abortive woman. In this chapter, we will discuss who the post-abortive woman is, what she has been through, why she is hiding, and the potential impact of her story. As you read, I pray that you will begin to realize that women who have experienced abortion are all around us. If you don't know anyone who openly talks about her abortion, that doesn't mean no one in your life has had an abortion. Most are hiding their stories and their pain.

Who is the Post-Abortive Woman?

As mentioned in chapter 5, women of all ages, ethnicities, backgrounds, education levels, and church experience have had abortions. That means, women of all ages, ethnicities, backgrounds, education levels, and church experience are dealing with the soul-wounds abortion causes.

I want to revisit the 2015 study by CareNet mentioned previously, which revealed that 70 percent of women getting abortions indicate they are Christians. One-third of those women said they attend church one or more times each week.[1] It's tempting to believe that post-abortive women aren't part of our church families but that simply isn't true. There is no doubt about it, there are women hiding the pain of abortion sitting in the pews of every church in our country.

1. "Abortion in Church." 32.

The first time I shared my abortion experience with a friend, I expected her to be shocked and possibly angry with me, but I was surprised by her response. She was in tears because she realized that even though she was pro-life and volunteered with a pregnancy care center, she was terribly misinformed about women who have had abortions. She told me I changed her view of post-abortive women because she had never imagined someone like me would make that choice. Suddenly she looked at those with abortions in their past differently. She no longer saw them as someone she couldn't relate to, someone far removed from herself. It became easier for her to show these women grace and to love them even though she doesn't agree with the choice they made.

Once we can relate to the women who have made this choice and rip away all our false assumptions about them, it will be much easier for us to remember that each and every woman, who has chosen abortion, was made in the image of God, and is STILL loved by Him. In fact, God loves them just as much after their abortions as He did the day He breathed life into them.

> "And I am convinced that nothing can ever separate us from God's love. Neither death nor life, neither angels nor demons, neither our fears for today nor our worries about tomorrow—not even the powers of hell can separate us from God's love." Romans 8:38 (NLT)

This verse does not exclude women who have chosen abortion. God loves His children regardless of their choices therefore, our ability to see the post-abortive as God's children is imperative in the fight for life.

That same chapter in Romans also says, "So there is now no condemnation for those who belong to Christ Jesus." (Romans 8:1 NLT) According to this verse, those who believe in Jesus and know His sacrifice is their only hope for salvation, are not condemned for their choice to abort, or for any other choices they've made or will ever make.

Because of this truth, we can determine that post-abortive women are loved by God and not condemned by Him. He deems them valuable, but these women cannot

> Once we can relate to women who have made this choice and rip away all our false assumptions about them, it will be much easier for us to remember that each and every woman who has chosen abortion was made in the image of God, and is still loved by Him.

see that for themselves. They have believed the lie from Satan that they will never be loved, forgiven, or worth God's time.

One time while picking up a prescription, the technician asked for my driver's license and then placed it inside a little envelope and stapled the envelope to the prescription bag. When I got home, I took the pill bottle out and threw the bag in the trash. Later I noticed my driver's license wasn't in my purse so I started digging through the trash, looking for my missing ID. I looked in all the small trash cans throughout the house because I couldn't remember where I had thrown the prescription bag. Then, I pushed up my sleeves and searched through the kitchen trash can. Sadly, I couldn't find it anywhere inside the house so, I started pulling out trash bags from the big garbage can outside. It was a smelly, yucky mess. I ended up with ketchup all over my hands, food on my shirt, and trash all over the yard. I pulled out every single piece of paper, snack wrapper, and banana peel.

Finally, I found it. It was in the very last bag at the bottom of the big brown trash can. I cleaned up the mess, put all the bags back in the garbage can, and put my license back where it belonged, in my purse.

As I did all of this, I couldn't help but see similarities in what God has done and continues to do for His children. When we are lost, He determines to find us. Even when the hunt is gross and dirty. Even when we continue to run from Him, He looks in place after place. He never stops pursuing us, until we are found. He never gives up on us. He pulls us out of the trash and places us right where we belong, with Him.

This applies all of God's children, including those who have had abortions. God willingly pursues them. He faithfully continues searching until they are found. It's our Heavenly Father's desire to have all His children close to Him, no matter how long it takes.

So, who is the post-abortive woman? She is someone that is loved by God, valuable to God, and pursued by God. She is someone who made a terrible choice, possibly more than once. She is a sinner, just like you and me. But just like every other sinner, if she surrenders to Jesus and believes He is her savior, she is forgiven of all her sins, including abortion.

What Has She Been Through?

Unless it's a personal experience or something we've witnessed first-hand, I don't believe it's possible for anyone to truly relate with a woman who has made the choice to abort. Therefore, I want to shed light on what many post-abortive women have dealt with during and after their abortions.

As covered in chapter 5, women who have abortions are traumatized by discovering the pregnancy and by the process of making the decision to abort, all of which will be followed by a terribly traumatic abortion experience.

Abortion is considered a medical procedure, but it's unlike any other. Women who are less than ten weeks pregnant are allowed the opportunity to choose a medical abortion, which involves taking a drug called Mifepristone in the doctor's office, followed by ingesting Misoprostol at home. Women endure the process of this abortion at home, all alone.

In a 2021 Live Action article Kristen said, "*About an hour after taking the pill [Misoprostol], I felt nauseous. I went to the bathroom and started violently throwing up. I felt dizzy and lightheaded. I couldn't stop puking. Then, the bleeding started. And it was nothing like a heavy period.*" To deal with all the blood, Kristen decided to get into the shower, and soon, the body parts of her baby began to leave her womb. "*I definitely saw an arm (and even fingers),*" she said. "*It was so tiny. Everything came out in pieces, though. It mostly looked like blood clots, but I could still make out parts. I just tried my best not to look and wash it all away as quickly as possible.*" The pain Kristen experienced was unbearable. She called the clinic's phone number to ask for assistance and was told to take ibuprofen, which did not lessen her pain. "*At one point, I passed out in the shower. I woke up in a pool of blood with freezing cold water pouring on my feet. I tried to crawl out of the bathroom, but I could only make it a few feet before just giving up and laying down on the cold bathroom floor, completely naked,*" Kristen said. "*I bled for weeks; they didn't warn me about that,*" she said.[2]

The abortion pill is advertised as any easy way to end a pregnancy; an option that is completed in the comfort of your own home, while the uterus is gently emptied, like a heavy period. Kristen's experience, like so many other women I've spoken with, was anything but gentle. A medical abortion is physically painful and emotionally tragic. It is a terribly traumatic experience. Surgical abortions are no different.

A vacuum aspiration abortion is a procedure in which metal rods are used to dilate the cervix, a suction catheter is used to forcibly pull the baby from the mother's womb, followed by tools which scrape the uterine lining to ensure everything was removed. This is a very painful experience; I know because I had this type of abortion when I was sixteen years old. I was not

2. Shaw, "Emotional Agony." 10.

given any sedation or calming medications; nor was I given anything to help with the pain. I was, however, told to be still, stop shaking, and be quiet throughout the procedure, as the abortionist joked that she didn't want to miss anything. While enduring tremendous pain caused by an apathetic old woman, who was obviously in a rush, I also heard the sounds of suction and scraping, which haunted me for years.

D&E abortions occur during the second trimester. Dilation and Evacuation is a surgical procedure involving the use of laminaria to open the woman's cervix. Laminaria is a type of seaweed that is inserted into the cervix twenty-four to forty-eight hours prior to the abortion appointment. A suction catheter is used to empty the womb of amniotic fluid and then a sopher clamp is used to grasp the baby, pulling it apart, and removing it, piece by piece from the uterus. The abortionist then reassembles the body parts to ensure everything has been removed.

Induction abortions happen during the third trimester and are a three- or four-day process. On day one, the abortionist injects the baby with a lethal dose of Digoxin or Potassium Chloride, which causes fetal cardiac arrest and ends the life of the child. Laminaria is also inserted in the cervix. On day two, the abortionist uses an ultrasound to ensure the baby is dead, replaces the laminaria, and gives the woman labor-inducing medications. The woman returns home and waits for her body to dilate enough to deliver her dead baby. On day three or four, the woman goes back to the clinic for delivery. If she goes into labor while at home, she is advised to sit on the toilet until the abortionist arrives. If the baby is delivered before the abortionist arrives, he or she will come to clean up and remove the baby from the home. If the child is not delivered whole, the procedure changes to a D&E.

After reading the truth about abortion procedures, can you agree that abortion is a traumatic experience? Most women have been told that abortion is their best option; a choice which will allow their lives to go back to normal. I'm not sure anyone could go back to normal after experiencing any of those procedures.

Not only do these women suffer from the trauma associated with the abortion itself, but there are also many things following an abortion that are traumatic. There is often a feeling of relief after abortion, time in denial about the whole thing, and then women begin feeling swallowed up by shame and guilt. As their minds clear and they begin to realize what they've done, a host of symptoms can occur.

As noted in the first chapter of this book, post-abortive women deal with regret, depression, numbness, self-loathing, self-harm, fear of God's punishment, self-medicating, nightmares, flashbacks, poor self-image, fear of losing living children, preoccupation with replacing the aborted child, anniversary syndrome, and suicidal thoughts/attempts, among others.

For a mother, the weight of knowing she took the life of her own child is almost unbearable. She is faced with the realization that a child in the womb should be protected but she chose to harm it. She is confronted by the fact that she robbed her living children of a sibling. She realizes she is responsible for the hurtful affects her choice to abort has on her family.

Women also often suffer from PASS (Post-Abortion Stress Syndrome). PASS is the name given to the psychological aftereffects of abortion. This syndrome is like PTSD (Post-Traumatic Stress Disorder) because any event that causes trauma can lead to PTSD, abortion included.

In many cases, these women feel deceived and forgotten. The abortion industry insisted this was an easy way out; a choice she would be glad she made. People in her life encouraged her to make this decision, explaining that they were being supportive or possibly pressuring her to go to the clinic. It seemed like an acceptable option since it was her legal right to make the choice. But later, when she is drowning in her regret, there is no one to help her. There is no one for her to talk to. Abortion clinics do not provide therapy or resources for those who have experienced this traumatic event. She has heard pro-life advocates condemning women who have chosen abortion and swears she will never tell anyone what she's done. No one talks about regretting the decision, so she begins to wonder if she is the only one who wishes she hadn't chosen to abort. She refuses to acknowledge the little life she took because she knows it will cause her to grieve and she doesn't believe she deserves to do even that. She feels she has nowhere to go, no one to talk to, and no hope that she'll ever feel any different. She is filled with a constant, silent scream that only she can hear.

Why Is She Hiding?

One might wonder, if post-abortive women regret their choice and hope others don't make the same mistake, why don't more of them speak up?

As mentioned previously, most post-abortive women are struggling with a myriad of emotional symptoms, of which shame is the ringleader. Shame is different than guilt. Guilt reminds us that we made a mistake.

Shame tells us that we *are* a mistake. Women covered in shame have begun to believe the lie that they are the worst decision they've ever made. They believe they will never be more than a failure. They cannot envision themselves as successful, valuable, loved, or wanted. Even if they have the desire to help abortion-vulnerable women make a different choice and speak out against abortion, shame is a giant that crowds their thinking. It tells them they cannot do it, should not do it, and if they do, everyone will hate them or laugh at them.

As believers, we know the cure for disabling shame. Jesus Christ wants to pick these ladies up, wipe away the tears, and remove every ounce of shame. He wants to replace it with His strength and peace. He wants to take their stories and turn them into something magnificent and purposeful. He knew the choices they would make, and He still has a plan for their lives.

One of Satan's goals is to keep us from fulfilling the purpose God designed for us. With post-abortive men and women, the enemy thinks he's succeeded. He uses shame and other emotional struggles to keep us in a place of despair. He doesn't want us to realize that God still loves us or that God desires for us to live a beautiful and abundant life. He uses deception to cause us to doubt any progress we've made, and whispers lies to keep us on the hamster wheel of discouragement and fear.

It's also important to note that while these women are often silent, they are not missing. They may not talk about abortion but any time the topic is brought up, their ears perk up. They may want to run from the conversation but since that would cause people to wonder, they just listen intently. They hear every judgement, critical statement, and hateful assumption. They are entirely aware of how much of the pro-life community looks down upon women who have had abortions. They have heard comments like, "How could a woman do such a thing, she must be a monster." "Women who have had abortions are murderers and deserve to live with their guilt." "God hates murderers." "There is no way

> *Between the shame they are already experiencing and the condemnation they expect to receive from others, it's not surprising that a post-abortive woman would keep her pain and experiences a secret. It feel safer to hide it and pretend like everything is fine.*

I could forgive someone that aborted my family member." "Women who chose abortion are simply selfish."

These are real comments made by real pro-life supporters, heard by real post-abortive participants in the abortion recovery groups I lead. While there may be some truth in those statements, they are not helpful in any way. These degrading comments are not easily forgotten, and they often keep women who have experienced abortion from seeking help or speaking up about their experience because they fear the judgement of those who fight for life.

Between the shame they are already experiencing and the condemnation they expect to receive from others, it's not surprising that a post-abortive woman would keep her pain and experiences a secret. It feels safer to hide it and pretend like everything is fine.

What Impact Could She Have?

Imagine for a moment that you are planning a trip to a remote island. All your research has revealed gorgeous, shimmering beaches and a beautiful historic city. You've read reviews praising the luxurious accommodations and incredible snorkeling experiences. You've seen countless photos of the tropical paradise and enjoyed stories about the island-life vibes. Based on all you've read and observed, you believe this trip may be the best vacation ever. You are excited about hiking the volcanoes and immersing yourself in the laid-back culture. You're looking forward to basking in the sun, eating delicious food, and relaxing by the crystal-clear water. You even have friends who are jealous of this trip because they've heard it is the most beautiful place in the world, somewhere they would go, if they could.

Now pretend you mention this upcoming vacation to an acquaintance who went on a similar trip eighteen months prior. Upon hearing the news about your plans to visit this specific island, all the color drains from his face and tears begin to trickle down his cheeks. He quietly shares the story of his vacation to the beautiful island. He confirms how lovely the scenery is and shares how remarkable his resort had been. He explains that he and his wife were just as excited as you, for their vacation there.

Then, he begins to speak of the nightmare they experienced while laying on padded beach chairs near the pristine coastline. His wife had decided to take a dip in the ocean, but he chose to stay in his comfortable spot. He dozed off a little as he listened to the waves crashing. He woke to the screams of his wife. Immediately, he jumped up, startled by the desperation in her voice. He saw a group of men grabbing his wife, dragging her into a hut nearby. He chased after them, yelling for them to let her go. The door to the hut had been blocked, refusing him entry. He could hear the cries of his beloved wife. She was being raped and tortured by these horrible men. He screamed for help as he ran toward the resort. He begged for someone to save his wife but everyone he encountered couldn't understand him. He rushed back to the hut only to find that it was empty. The men had kidnapped the love of his life and they were nowhere to be found.

He explains that he sought help, but the natives made light of his situation; it seems this sort of thing happens often there. He called home for assistance but there was very little they could do. A friend began to do research and discovered information about similar incidents in the area and reported back to him that a terrorist group in the area had been known to attack westerners and hold them for ransom.

He continued sharing more details of the experience, finally revealing that his wife had been returned to him after weeks of grueling negotiations. It took all their life savings to retrieve his usually delightful wife, but when she returned, she was only a shell of who she used to be. Her smile was different. She pretended she was okay, but the traumatic experience had done its damage and she was no longer the same person. She was embarrassed and depressed. She didn't want to speak about the events because it was too painful. It seemed people all around her whispered about her and she felt completely alone. The experience impacted every aspect of her life, strained their marriage, and negatively affected their family in many ways.

He also explained that incidents like the one his wife endured occur frequently on the island, but because the native people rely heavily on tourism, the truth was concealed. The government officials, resort owners, and other important businessmen made an agreement to keep the truth about these attacks and kidnappings a secret to ensure tourists would continue visiting the island.

The pain in his face as he shared this story was evidence that it was true. His vivid recollection of the event tore at your heart and gripped you with fear. Suddenly, the exotic island didn't seem so picturesque. Everything you originally read about the vacation spot made it seem safe and appealing, but his first-hand experience changed your thoughts about the vacation entirely. Once you heard his story and learned of the on-going attacks on westerners, your opinion about the island changed and you decided not to visit there.

Abortion is no vacation, but I believe the comparisons between this story and abortion are easily noted. Abortion is portrayed as simple safe, and consequence free. Much like the tropical island in the story, until someone who has experienced abortion shares their first-hand experience, it is often viewed as a great option. But when a woman, wounded by abortion, shares what she endured and the impact abortion has had on her life, it changes things. When someone hears a first-hand report, revealing the truth about abortion, they can no longer only recall what they've read or been told by the abortion industry. Once they've heard the story of someone who has been inside the clinic, the lies begin to unravel and the truth about abortion is uncovered.

Men and women who have experienced abortion have stories that need to be told. They can share the trauma they suffered and the horrific experiences they barely survived. They can shed light on the damage abortion caused in their lives and in the lives of their family members, as well as the emotional turmoil they continue to endure.

The ones who have walked in the shoes of those considering abortion are the only ones who can truly understand what abortion-vulnerable women are facing. They are the only ones who can say, "I've been where you are, and I understand what you're going through." They are also the only ones that can truthfully share the impact abortion has and the regret that plagues them. Those considering abortion will also feel the most comfortable conversing with someone they view as nonjudgmental, and since post-abortive men and women have had abortions, they are viewed as safe people to talk to.

Post-abortive men and women could potentially make the most impact in the fight against abortion because they can go places no one other pro-life advocate can go when talking to abortion-vulnerable women or about abortion in general.

So, who are post-abortive women? They are the greatest weapon in the fight against abortion but most of them choose to hide. They have been silenced by shame, fear of judgment, and condemnation.

7

How Should We Respond?

IN THE LAST TWO chapters we discussed who abortion-vulnerable and post-abortive women are. We've also become aware of all they have endured and why they may have chosen abortion or be considering one. So, now we must ask ourselves, how should we respond to the women who find themselves in a desperate situation? What should we say or do to help the ladies who have been carrying the weight of shame and guilt after abortion?

It's important to note that our correct response is multi-faceted. To truly help these women and positively impact the fight for life, our attitudes, and the way we talk about the topic of abortion, are just as important as the way speak to the women entering an abortion clinic.

Abortion is a topic that has affected or will affect more people than we can imagine. Before and after an abortion is committed, women are listening and are completely aware of the posture held by the pro-life movement. Like we mentioned previously, "one bad apple can ruin the bunch." Even if there are many advocates who embody compassion and love toward the abortion-vulnerable and post-abortive; they are often hidden behind those who loudly scold and judge. So, it's vitally important for us to respond in love.

In this chapter, we will discuss the many layers that make up an appropriate and helpful response to women who are considering abortion or have had one.

Our Walk

The way someone lives reveals a lot about them. It's not hard to determine if someone actually "walks the talk." Through observation we decide if they are trustworthy, authentic, truthful, dependable, patient, or kind. Even if someone says they will keep a secret, if we notice them gossiping about others, we know their words are not truthful and deduce that they are not trustworthy. Therefore, I believe the way we walk through life plays a significant role when someone is deciding if we are trustworthy or dependable enough to confide in.

> "As a prisoner for the Lord, then, I urge you to live a life worthy of the calling you have received." Ephesians 4:1(NIV)

You may ask, what is the calling I've received? God has different plans and purposes for each of us, but one incredible calling we all have in common can be found in Ephesians 3:10(NLT), which says, "God's purpose in all this was to use the church to display His wisdom in its rich variety to all the unseen rulers and authorities in the heavenly places."

This verse declares that God's purpose for the church (His people) is to display His wisdom to all the unseen authorities in the heavenly places. That means, God uses us, His people, to reveal things even to the angels. He uses us, the physical, to teach the supernatural. How amazing is that? Not only is the church called to love others and make disciples, but we are also used by God to teach the angels more about Him.

If we're called to teach the angels of God's goodness and wisdom, we can easily infer that we are also called to teach those around us about God. He wants to use us, the physical, to reveal spiritual things to others. That is an incredible calling! A calling that all believers have in common.

In Ephesians 4:1, Paul urges us to live a life that seems impossible, and while we will fail from time to time, we should aim to live in such a way that is worthy of that calling. We should live a life that points others to God (1 Peter 2:12 NIV) and is proof that God's promises are yes and amen (2 Corinthians 1:20 NIV).

How do we live that kind of life? I believe it starts with humility and surrender. When we realize that we are unable to live a life worthy of the calling and ask God to help us, He is right there to bolster us. We must not forget that His love and acceptance are never based on how well we perform or what we do. His mercy and grace are continuous, so even when we mess up, He remains with us, offering Himself to us.

Jesus also tells us in John 15 that He will send a Helper; the Spirit of Truth that comes from the Father. Being aware of this Helper and allowing Him to work in and through us, makes all the difference. We must acknowledge the Holy Spirit and ask Him to fill us and guide us. When we do, Galatians 5:22–23 tells us that we will bear much good fruit.

> "But the fruit of the Spirit is love, joy, peace, patience, kindness, goodness, faithfulness, gentleness, and self-control. Against such things there is no law." Galatians 5:22–23 (NIV)

If those are the fruits of the Spirit, the fruits of darkness probably include their opposites such as: anger, confusion, manipulation, critical attitudes, complaining, lying, irritability, impatience, boasting, hatred, selfishness, harshness, promise breaking, and a lack of self-control.

It's not hard to believe that while the fruit of the Spirit draws people in, the fruits of darkness push people away. We all probably know someone who is obviously filled with the Holy Spirit and exudes those beautiful fruits. You can probably also think of someone who displays the characteristics of darkness. Who would you rather be around?

Which of these fruits manifest when we humbly walk in surrender to God, aiming to live a life worthy of our calling? With the Helper's assistance, the fruit of the Spirit will radiate from within us and will be a gift to those around us.

I also believe integrity is of the highest importance for believers. In my house we define integrity as doing the right thing, even when no one is watching.

> The integrity of the upright guides them, but the unfaithful are destroyed by their duplicity. Proverbs 11:3 (NIV)

It's not enough to pretend to live a life worthy of our calling, just so other's think wonderful things about us. We need do the right thing, even when others aren't watching. If not, the truth will eventually be exposed, and it will destroy us. When that occurs, it can greatly impact those around us and cause people to believe that all Christians are untrustworthy and hypocritical.

It's sobering to think that sinners are part of God's plan for the salvation of the World. Jesus gave His life for everyone, and God uses us as His vehicle for bringing awareness of that truth to unbelievers. We aren't alone in this great task. The Helper is with us, guiding us, and equipping us. But the Holy Spirit only uses those who are humble enough to be used. If we are looking down on others and consider ourselves better than someone else, we cannot also be humble. The Holy Spirit wants to speak through us to those in need. What the Holy Spirit says will be different for every person and in each situation. If we already have our speeches and condemning statements prepared, it will be impossible for Him to speak through us.

In addition, we must remember that faith and control are opposites. If we are trying to control situations, people, or outcomes, we don't also have faith. If loss of control causes us to panic and feel hopeless, we are not filled with faith.

> "Now faith shows the reality of what we hope for and it is the evidence of what we cannot see." Hebrews 11:1 (NIV)

If faith means we are sure and certain about things we hope for and things we can't even see, we can surmise that faith also means to release control entirely and trust that God will take care of it all.

If we believe the wind and waves obey Him, that He can raise people from the dead, and that He created everyone and everything, we should act like it. We carry that out by releasing our clutch on people and situations in our lives, by putting an end to our tendency to manipulate circumstances, and by choosing to have faith.

> *What the Holy Spirit says will be different for every person and in each situation. If we already have our speeches and condemning statements prepared, it will be impossible for Him to speak through us.*

People of integrity who are humble, filled with the Holy Spirit, full of faith, and aiming to live a life worthy of their calling are trustworthy, approachable, and gentle. These characteristics have an enormous impact on the opinion abortion-vulnerable and post-abortive women have of us and how they will receive us. It will also affect their willingness to come to us for help in a time of need.

Our Words and Actions

Abortion is a controversial topic and one that many are extremely passionate about, on both sides. Abortion makes pro-life advocates angry, and we want to do something about it!

I believe, however, in order to make the most impact for life, we must remember something my mom always says, "You'll catch more flies with honey than vinegar." Regardless of our intentions, our words and actions are often enveloped by the stench of vinegar and become a hinderance in the fight against abortion.

A person's views about God aren't formed in one day, or even one year. Our view of God is shaped by a multitude of things. Our relationships with our earthly fathers, influences by other believers, lessons we've been taught, times Christians have hurt us, ways we've been blessed by believers, things we've heard about believers, the Bible, and the attitudes of those we encounter at church, as well as many other things, all help to form our view of God.

Therefore, we must realize the way we speak to non-believers, or believers who have strayed, could greatly impact their view the church and God. While we may feel it's important to make sure sinners realize their sin, the truth is, we are not God. We are not called to convict others. That is the Holy Spirit's role. We are called to love others the way Jesus loves us. We mustn't forget that we were once in need of grace, and we still are! Jesus showed us mercy and grace and loved us even though we were in an ugly place. Since we are called to love others the way Jesus loves us, then we need to show them grace, mercy, and unconditional love.

Seeds are being planted throughout our day-to-day lives. We aren't always aware of them, but God is always planting things within us, with the hope that they will grow and become fruitful. Our enemy, Satan, is attempting to plant things in our lives as well, hoping those things will take root, sprout, and cause disruption and chaos.

Even before someone is saved, seeds are being planted that have the potential to help them grow into a relationship with Christ or cause them to push Christ away. As God's children, we are often the ones God uses to plant seeds in the lives of others. We must be aware of how we are speaking and remain mindful of our attitudes. Whether it be about contentious topics like abortion and homosexuality, or a somewhat safer topic, we need to seek the Holy Spirit's direction before we speak. Our words and actions are like seeds planted in the lives of others. We don't want what we say or how we treat someone to grow into something that causes them to doubt God, believe He hates them, or continue hiding in their sin instead of allowing God to free them.

Since we know one in four women have an abortion in their lifetime, we can be sure that there are post-abortive women (and men) in our churches, places of employment, neighborhoods, and even in our families. There are people all around us that have experienced an abortion and are keeping it a secret. There are also young girls and women who will soon face an unplanned pregnancy. Therefore, we must have control over our tongues and watch our words about this topic. What we say may cause a woman to believe she should never speak of her experience, or it could give her the courage to finally say speak up because she believes others care about her and God forgives her. It may cause a woman to seek help when she discovers she's pregnant, or it could cause her to run to a clinic so she can hide her sin.

> "Death and life are in the power of the tongue." Proverbs 18:21a (ESV)

In this case, this verse couldn't be more applicable. Our words and actions can literally play a part in the life or death of a preborn child. We can also play a part in whether a person accepts the gift of eternal life or believes she/he can live an abundant life, a life of freedom and wholeness.

How many women are simply afraid to speak of their unplanned pregnancies or past abortions because they fear what others will say? Sadly, fear of what others will think and say is one of the main reasons women stay in hiding, especially Christians. That fear has most likely developed in part because of what they've heard others say about pregnancy out of wedlock, abortion, and/or post-abortive women.

It's also worth pointing out that what we post on social media is just as important as the words that come out of our mouths. A young lady, who attended one of my post-abortion Bible study groups, was terrified of what a family member would say if she was open about her past abortion. Her fear was based entirely on what that family member had posted on social media about abortion. We can share our opinion on the matter and bring awareness about the topic without being hateful, judgmental, and condemning. I believe it's vital that we make a conscious effort to do so.

> "The Lord is gracious and righteous; our God is full of compassion." Psalm 116:5 (NIV)

This verse says that God is full of compassion. That means in the moments a woman is sitting on her bathroom floor in tears, holding a positive pregnancy test; God is full of compassion for her. When she is being pressured to abort by a boyfriend or parent; God is full of compassion for her. When she calls the abortion clinic; God is full of compassion for her. Even when she's laying on the table; God is full of compassion for her. When she walks out the door of the clinic; God is full of compassion for her. As she struggles with self-hatred, shame, and depression for years following her choice; God is full of compassion for her.

God sees her. He knows what she is experiencing. He also knows the other factors in her life that she is trying to balance. He doesn't look at her with disgust or disappointment. He looks at her with compassion and love. Even as the procedure is taking place, God is looking at His beloved daughter, saying, "Precious girl, don't make this choice, this is going to cause you so much pain."

"Be imitators of me, as I am of Christ." 1 Corinthians 11:1 (ESV)

If we are called to be imitators of Christ, we need to be full of compassion for women considering abortion and those who have had one. Seeking justice and being angry about abortion is normal and to be expected, but if we are to imitate Christ, our compassion must supersede our anger and we must control our tongues. If not, we risk acting like a Pharisee—caring more about the law and religion than the person Jesus came to rescue.

This is true when speaking directly to an abortion-vulnerable or postabortive woman, but it's also true when speaking about this topic in general. As mentioned previously, these women are all around us. They are listening to us, watching us, and reading our posts. They are continually determining who is trustworthy, who is judgmental, and who is authentic.

Often, the "essence" of who we are is what people remember or recall when they think about us. Did we make them feel loved and noticed or did we cause them to feel judged and ridiculed? Do they feel safe with us? Did we seem genuine? Were we pushy and opinionated or caring and peaceful? What they recall about people helps them decide who they can trust if they discover their pregnant, or who they can talk to when they're covered in shame.

As imitators of Christ, our "essence" should be like His: sweet, loving, calming, peaceful, chain-breaking, freedom-bringing, and approachable.

Consider the story of the prodigal son in the book of Luke, chapter 15. A selfish son ran off with his inheritance, believing it was a great idea, but ended up blowing it and eating dinner out of a pig trough. He reluctantly decided to go back home, just hoping his father would let him be a worker. At least that way he would have decent food to eat.

The father (representing God) ran out to meet the son. He was not standing by the door with his hands on his hips and a stern look on his face. He was not calling out all the sin in his son's life. Instead, he was there with wide open arms. He was joyful about his son's return. He told his servants to get a robe and a ring for his son because he wanted to celebrate his return and clothe him in the best possible things.

As people of God, we are called to help people find their way to God, or back to God when they've run away. If the prodigal son is a picture of what God has designed for those who have strayed, who are we to dampen that with our judgements and opinions?

Our words, actions, and attitudes play a substantial role in our response to women who have had abortions or are considering one. Yes, these people have sinned. Yes, they are vulnerable and have the potential to make a terrible choice. But we must be careful, or we may end up being unwanted, noisy bystanders in the story God is writing in their lives. He is welcoming them, loving them, and showing them grace and mercy. He doesn't need or want us to callously call out the sins of His child while He attempts to bring that child home. If we do that, we could potentially cause the person to run further away. They may connect our words to the Father and believe He feels the same way we do. They may believe God will scold them because we do. They may never return because of our insensitive attitudes toward them.

> "Honor me by trusting in me in your day of trouble. Cry aloud to me, and I will be there to rescue you." Psalm 50:15 (TPT)

When we are overwhelmed, God wants us to come to Him. The same is true for those facing an unplanned pregnancy and those drowning in sorrow. So, as God's people, we need to be welcoming; always inviting them in. We don't want things we've said or done, or our bad attitudes to be the reason people do not come to the Father.

Our Love

The most important thing we can do in response to all we've discussed about abortion-vulnerable and post-abortive women, is to love them. In fact, the Bible says loving one another should be our way of life.

> "Those who are loved by God, let His love continually pour from you to one another, because God is love. Everyone who loves is fathered by God and experiences an intimate knowledge of Him. The one who doesn't love has yet to know God, for God is love. The light of God's love shined within us when he sent His matchless Son into the world so that we might live through Him. This is love: He loved us *long before we loved Him*. It was His love, not ours. He proved it by sending his Son to be the pleasing sacrificial offering to take away our sins. Delightfully loved ones, if He loved us with such tremendous love, then "loving one another" should be our way of life! No one has ever gazed upon the fullness of God's splendor. But if we love one another, God makes His permanent home in us, and we make our permanent home in Him, and His love is brought to its full expression in us. And He has given us His Spirit within us so that we can have the assurance that He lives in us and that we live in Him. Moreover, we have seen with our own eyes and can testify to the truth that Father God has sent His Son to be the Savior of the world. Those who give thanks that Jesus is the Son of God live in God, and God lives in them. We have come into an intimate experience with God's love, and we trust in the love He has for us. God is love! Those who are living in love are living in God, and God lives through them. By *living in God*, love has been brought to its full expression in us so that we may fearlessly face the day of judgment, because all that Jesus now is, so are we in this world. Love never brings fear, for fear is always related to punishment. But love's perfection drives the fear *of punishment far* from our hearts. Whoever walks constantly afraid of *punishment* has not reached love's perfection. Our love for others is *our grateful response* to the love God first demonstrated to us. Anyone can say, "I love God," yet have hatred toward another believer. This makes him a phony, because if you don't love a brother or sister, whom you can see, how can you truly love God, whom you can't see? For he has given us this command: whoever loves God must also demonstrate love to others." 1 John 4:5–21 (TPT)

This passage says, "Our love for others is our grateful response to the love God first demonstrated to us." Sometimes it can feel unnatural and extremely difficult to love those who we strongly disagree with, those who have hurt us, or those whose actions are harming others. But when we recall the way God has loved us, even before we loved Him, it's easier to choose love towards others, in appreciation for the love we have received. Our love for others should be a response to God's love for us.

Gratitude for God's love and presence in our own lives, is necessary to continually choose to love others. This gratitude manifests when we intentionally remind ourselves that we, too, are sinners and have been saved by God's grace and mercy. We need to remind ourselves of all the ways He has blessed us, protected us, and led us. We should refuse to forget who we used to be and how God has redeemed, restored, and recreated us. His great love took us from death to life. If not for His grace, it may have been us standing in the very shoes of those we choose not to love.

It's also important to note that God "loved us *long before we loved Him*." (1 John 4:10 TPT). I am always touched by the fact that, "While we were still sinners, Christ died for us." (Romans 5:8b NIV) God looked at us and said, "I want her anyway, because I love her, and I know her potential."

Changing has never been a prerequisite for God's love and it shouldn't be a prerequisite for our love either. The Bible does not say we should love someone only after they have stopped sinning or once they've changed. We are called to love. Period.

God's love also doesn't discriminate. Because of His great kindness, God gives breath and life to all humans, even those who are evil. He loves the righteous and the unrighteous. (Matthew 5:45 NIV) God has decided that there is no unlovable person. If God loves everyone, so should we.

Some Christians believe it's our job to make sure others know how unhappy God is with their choices. When we do that, those people see a God of hate and malice. They're encouraged to think of God as a just an ornery judge with a gavel in His hand. They believe God hates them personally. But 1 John 4:8b (NIV) says, "God is love." If God is love, He cannot also be hate.

> Sometimes the greatest act of love is telling someone they're wrong, but how we do that is just as important as the message we're trying to convey.

Sometimes the greatest act of love is telling someone they're wrong, but how we do that is just as important as the message we're trying to convey. If we lovingly bring something to someone's attention, they may not like it, but they are less likely to believe they are hated by God and His people. If we are hateful and accusatory, and point out the worst in someone, they will feel judged, condemned, and unwanted by us and by God.

We need to be aware that most people know how sinful their lifestyle and choices are, they've just accepted it because they don't see another way. Love says, "I cannot watch you do to this to yourself, so I have to step in." Love says, "God wants so much more for you. Let me help you." Love does not say, "You're awful, what you're doing is awful, and when you change, I'll consider helping you even though you're awful."

God is the heart-changer. We need to let Him do what He does best.

> "Anyone who sets himself up as "religious" by talking a good game is self-deceived. This kind of religion is hot air and only hot air. Real religion, the kind that passes muster before God the Father, is this: Reach out to the homeless and loveless in their plight, and guard against corruption from the godless world." James 1:26–27 (MSG)

One of the purest demonstrations of God's love is to be aware of difficult situations and broken people and willingly choose to move towards them, instead of running away. It's tempting to turn our backs to hard circumstances or sticky situations and simply not get involved. It's also tempting to keep those people at a distance or make it known that we believe they're wrong. But when we "turn a blind eye" or shout our opinions, it's like running away from those who need God's love the most. To have the greatest impact, we must run toward those who are broken, even if we disagree with them, even if they are making terrible choices, and even if the situation is complex and messy.

> "Think of it this way: If a man owns a hundred sheep and one lamb wanders away and is lost, won't he leave the ninety-nine grazing the hillside and thoroughly search for the one lost lamb? And if he finds his lost lamb, he rejoices over it, more than over the ninety-nine that never went astray. Now you should understand that it is never the desire of your heavenly Father that a single one of these little ones should be lost." Matthew 18:12–14 (TPT)

We learn from the parable of the lost sheep that even if only one sheep goes astray and gets lost because of his own choices, and even if it gets stuck in a fence or is laying a big muddy puddle somewhere, the shepherd would search for it and rejoice when he found it. Jesus explains that every single one is valued and loved by the shepherd. The same is true for all of us. We are all important to God, each and every one of us. He loves us and doesn't want any of us to be left behind, regardless of our choices. I believe we can also glean from this passage that love should not be inconvenienced by the needs of others, and it should never attempt to determine whether someone is worthy of it or not.

I want to be clear; I am not suggesting that we should accept someone's sin and pretend it's okay. To love and accept the sinner does not mean we must love and accept the sin. I'm simply encouraging us to love the way our Heavenly Father does. He sees us all at our worst but still chooses to run toward us and love us.

Jesus Is Our Example

> "Above all, keep loving one another earnestly, since love covers a multitude of sins." 1 Peter 4:8 (ESV)

More than anything else we could do in the fight for life, is love those wounded by abortion and those considering one. 1 Peter 4:8 (ESV) says that love covers a multitude of sins. We know this true because Jesus loved us all enough to lay down His life for us. The sacrifice He made covers all our sins. It's our love that draws others to Him.

> "I give you a new command: Love one another. Just as I have loved you, you must also love one another." John 13:34 (HCSB)

We are called to love others the way Jesus has loved us. He loves us not because He must, but because He chooses to. Even when it feels awkward or we just simply don't want to love someone, our love should be driven by God's love for us and our love for Him.

Christians should love better than anyone else because Jesus modeled love so well. Jesus' love did not condemn, ridicule, or look down upon others. He loved without expectation, exception, or expiration. Jesus loved people regardless of their ethnicity or age. He loved them regardless of the marital status, their job, or how much money they had. He didn't care how they were dressed or what they looked like. Where they were from or where they were going didn't stop His love. Jesus' love was not dependent on the person or their actions. Jesus' love didn't even change based on the person's thoughts of Him.

Jesus' love was radical. Even though it wasn't popular and others didn't understand it, He loved prostitutes, adulterers, tax collectors, the lame, the blind, doubters, the unclean, Samaritans, Gentiles, Jews, and even the Pharisees. The disciples were even shocked by the love Jesus had for everyone, but that didn't stop Jesus.

In John 8, the Pharisees brought a woman to Jesus who had been caught in the act of adultery and asked Him what they should do with her; after reminding Him that Moses' law says she should be stoned to death. Jesus replied, "Let anyone of you who is without sin be the first to throw a stone at her" (John 8:7b NIV). The men slowly walked away leaving woman and Jesus alone. He asked her if any of them had condemned her, and she said no. "'Then neither do I condemn you.' Jesus declared, 'Go now and leave your life of sin.'" (John 8:11 NIV)

Jesus didn't ignore the truth about the woman. He didn't condemn her, but He also didn't condone her sin. Instead, He confronted it with grace and love. He protected her and did not allow the men to judge and condemn her. Then, He told her to leave her life of sin.

Jesus looked at people and saw their potential instead of their sin. He wasn't okay with their sin, but He knew once they were in His presence, their sinful lifestyles would begin making them uncomfortable. He knew they wouldn't be able to stay in their sin if they were close to Him.

Jesus also loved others even when He knew they would mess up and hurt Him.

Consider Judas, the disciple who betrayed Jesus, and Peter, the disciple who denied Jesus. On the night of the last supper, Jesus already knew what both Judas and Peter would do in the hours to come. Even though He knew, He didn't force them to leave the table. They both still ate dinner with Him, and He still washed their feet. He treated them with kindness and love, regardless of the choices He knew they would make.

> "I tell you, Peter, before the rooster crows today, you will deny three times that you know me." Luke 22:34 (NIV)

Peter couldn't imagine what Jesus said was true but as predicted, the rooster crowed each time he denied Jesus. Even though Peter denied Him, Jesus forgave him and used him in mighty ways. Peter knew he was loved by Jesus and spent the rest of His life serving Him because of the mercy and grace Jesus showed him.

How many times do you think Peter heard the rooster crow after that? During that time, he probably heard the rooster every single day. That sound could have been a terrible trigger but instead, I believe the rooster served as a reminder of Jesus' love and forgiveness. I imagine every time he heard a rooster crow, Peter recalled how good Jesus had been to him.

It's my prayer that we will love others so well, that just the thought of the pro-life community will be a reminder of God's goodness and love.

Our Response

There are many layers that make up an appropriate and helpful response to women who are considering abortion or have had one. If we remember that we are called to live a life worthy of our calling and to love everyone like Jesus did, our responses will become welcoming and life-giving.

If it's still difficult for you to respond this way to those involved with abortion, I want to remind you that when you show love to them, you are showing love to God.

> "The King will reply, 'Truly I tell you, whatever you did for one of the least of these brothers and sisters of mine, you did for me.'"
> Matthew 25:40 (NIV)

It's not our job to determine who the "least of these" are. Jesus wants us to treat others with love and kindness, as if we are doing it for Him, because we are. These precious brothers and sisters matter to Him. So, even if you find it hard to speak with love and have a good attitude about this topic, do it anyway, for Jesus.

Our Reward

> "God always blesses those who are kind to the poor and helpless. They're the first ones God helps when they find themselves in any trouble. The Lord will preserve and protect them. They'll be honored and esteemed while their enemies are defeated." Psalm 41:1–2 (TPT)

God is fully aware of all that's going on here on earth. He is not blind to the atrocity of abortion or any of the other horrific things happening in our world. He understands what we are up against and knows that it isn't easy to respond the way He would. It blesses His heart when His children desire to imitate Jesus and love one another well, even when it's difficult.

Psalm 41 says that He blesses those who are kind to the poor and helpless. I believe that includes the post-abortive woman, the abortion-vulnerable woman, and all of those who are still blind to the truth of abortion. They are spiritually depleted, lost, hopeless, and helpless. When we love them and respond to them with kindness, God promises to bless us. When we find ourselves in trouble, He will help us. He will preserve and protect us. He will honor us and defeat our enemies.

We shouldn't respond in love simply because God will reward us but knowing He sees our effort, knows our hearts, uses our kind responses, and rewards us on top of it, is amazing!

8

The Love Tool Kit

THROUGHOUT THIS BOOK WE'VE discussed many reasons why it's necessary to Lead with Love when communicating about abortion. While we are filled to the brim with pro-life conviction, our pro-life compassion must triumph. This fight is not about simply winning an argument, it's about changing hearts and saving lives. This chapter will provide tools to help everyone in the pro-life movement make a positive impact for life.

How to Communicate about the Topic of Abortion

Many times, the way we say things matters much more than the words we say. Regardless of our message, the person listening will comprehend our words, no matter our intention, through a filter of their own experiences and beliefs. This is entirely true when discussing the topic of abortion. Emotions run high when this issue is brought up, so approaching it with gentleness and understanding is the only way to potentially sway someone's opinion about abortion.

The division about how to approach abortion is wide. To close the gap, love must be our greatest tool. Otherwise, we could quickly cause the divide to widen and deepen.

The division about how to approach abortion is wide. To close the gap, love must be our greatest tool. Otherwise, we could quickly cause the divide to widen and deepen.

Here are a few tools for your *"Love Tool Kit,"* to help you talk about abortion with friends and family, on social media, or with those who disagree with your view.

1. **Invite the Holy Spirit into the conversation.**

   As we talk about the topic of abortion in our everyday lives, it's important to pray before, during, and after our conversations. When we find ourselves thinking about this topic, let's ask God to search our thoughts and redirect any that are inappropriate. When we are about to discuss abortion with others, let's ask God to soften our attitudes and words so that we are a welcoming, safe person for others to talk to. During a conversation, let's ask the Holy Spirit to speak through us, as only He can. After a conversation, let's pray that God would use the discussion to help draw others closer to Him and to open their eyes to the truth about abortion.

   Inviting the Holy Spirit to speak to and through us will be our very best tool.

2. **Remember who the fight is really against; and who the victims are.**

   > "For our struggle is not against flesh and blood, but against the rulers, against the authorities, against the powers of this dark world and against the spiritual forces of evil in the heavenly realms." Ephesians 6:12 (NIV)

   The Bible makes it clear that while it may feel like we're fighting other people, our battle is really a spiritual one. Satan would love for us to view ourselves as superior to others, belittle one another, speak with disrespect, and be judgmental. Those actions and attitudes further his attempt to cause division. We must remember that our primary citizenship is the kingdom of heaven. We are here but a short time, with the goal of helping other sinners find salvation in Jesus so they too, can spend eternity in heaven. Satan uses many tricks and strategies in attempt to thwart our plans. When we are aware that we're fighting evil instead of people, it changes the way we fight.

"Be serious! Be alert! Your adversary the Devil is prowling around like a roaring lion, looking for anyone he can devour." 1 Peter 5:8 (HCSB)

Abortion's greatest victims are the babies whose lives are taken, but those who are blind to the truth of abortion are also victims of our adversary, the Devil. He prowls around, looking for someone to devour. He has used irrational and illogical ideas to confuse them which causes an inability for them to understand the sanctity of human life. Many of these people have had abortions themselves or have a connection to abortion in some way. I believe their bold, and often brazen ways of defending abortion, are attempts to talk themselves into believing what they did was okay. It's possible that because misery loves company and fighting for abortion will ensure they aren't alone in it. Whatever the underlining factor is, the enemy is the instigator.

Remembering those who fight for abortion are victims of our adversary doesn't excuse their behavior, but it will benefit us as we fight for life.

3. **Remember, we are all sinners.**

It's hard for humans to wrap our minds around it, but sin is all the same in God's eyes. We typically regard one sin worse than another but, there is no ranking system for sin. To God, anger, gossip, hypocrisy, judgmental attitudes, and abortion are all the same. That means being hateful to an abortion-vulnerable woman is just as bad as the sin she committed. Speaking about post-abortive women with disdain or wishing them ill-will, is as terrible as what she did. Judging those who are pro-abortion is the same as choosing abortion ourselves.

Isn't it interesting that other sins aren't publicly judged and pointed out the way abortion is? I've never seen anyone stand outside an obese person's house yelling and belittling him because he is a glutton. I've also never observed hateful posts on social media calling someone out for adultery. This is a weak comparison because abortion takes the life of another person, but the illustration makes perfect sense if we remember that God views all sin the same.

There are some folks in the pro-life movement, who claim they are Christ-followers, but say and post critical, hateful, belittling things about those who support abortion and/or have had one. What other sins do people feel haughty enough to talk about this way? What does this say about these pro-life individuals? What impression does it give others?

"For all have sinned and fall short of the glory of God." Romans 3:23 (ESV)

4. Remember your calling.

God saved us so we can help save others. He parted the seas of our sin so we could walk on dry land, so we could dance and sing and shout, and so that we could have an impact on those around us. He did not save us so we could be judgmental of those who seas aren't yet parted. Our most important duty of all is to walk in the *love* of God. It's important that we continually readjust our values and place first things first.

5. Decide who you are representing.

As Christians, it should be our desire to consistently and authentically represent Jesus. We will not succeed all the time but keeping our eyes on Jesus and aiming to imitate Him well, will allow others to see how beautiful being a Christian can be.

For those who are not Christ followers, when discussing the topic of abortion, you are representing the pro-life movement. Remember, "one bad apple ruins the bunch." I believe none of us want to be that bad apple. For us to make the greatest impact for life, we all need to be aware of what we represent.

6. Make a good first impression.

Our face is like a welcome mat to a conversation with us. If we are scowling and glaring at someone, it's like we're wearing a mat that says, "You aren't welcome here." On the other hand, a gentle, loving expression says, "It's safe to talk to me."

As Christians, we are not only recipients of God's love but also distributors of God's love. This should be evident in our actions, words, attitudes, and even our facial expressions. We only have one chance to make a good first impression. Chances are, if we come across as hateful or bitter, no one will want to discuss a topic like abortion with us, or any topic for that matter.

God is not harsh, hateful, unforgiving, or disrespectful. We must use our first impressions as opportunities to reveal that we aren't either.

7. **Promote love.**

When discussing abortion with others or sharing a post on social media about the topic, we are given the opportunity to show the world that Christ followers are different because of our love for God and our love for others.

> "Jesus replied: "'Love the Lord your God with all your heart and with all your soul and with all your mind. This is the first and greatest commandment. And the second is like it: 'Love your neighbor as yourself.'" Matthew 22:37–39 (NIV)

Love is not a gray area for believers. Jesus made it clear that love is the most important thing. We are to love God and love others. This means we should be conduits of the type of love that can cast out fear. We should be ministers of reconciliation. We should comfort others because we have been comforted.

8. **Be patient.**

Someone's opinions and ideas about abortion were most likely not formed in one day. Therefore, we will not be able to change someone's mind in one conversation. Being impatient will always push people away but patience and kindness may pave the way for multiple opportunities to talk with someone about this topic. In time, we may see a shift in their beliefs. Demanding someone change their way of thinking to match ours, in just a few minutes, is fruitless. We should remind ourselves that God uses these opportunities and builds upon them as He pursues him/her.

9. **Be a good listener.**

If we desire to understand someone's thoughts and ideas, we need to listen intentionally to what the other person is saying. If we take the time to truly hear them, they will be more likely to also listen to us and thoughtfully consider what we have to say.

It's also true that many people who call themselves pro-choice have been misinformed or are lacking vital information needed to form an appropriate opinion about abortion. If we listen closely, we may be able to impart truth that will make a difference in their opinion.

In addition, we should refrain from totally accepting one view and demonizing all other points of view. Doing so makes us bias. Christ-followers shouldn't behave this way because it keeps us from fully listening to one another. God places specific people in our path for us to plant seeds of truth within them. If we are bias and dismiss their thoughts and ideas, we will not hear their hearts and will miss the opportunity to do kingdom work.

10. **Turn away from disparaging attitudes.**

It's no simple task, but we must turn away from attitudes that are condescending or contemptuous. That behavior is not reflective of Jesus, but also, attitudes like these turn people away. If our goal is to help others see the truth about abortion and hopefully change their opinion, we must try to draw them in, not push them away.

I believe this is why so many pro-abortion advocates accuse the pro-life community of being hypocrites. When we point our fingers at others, wear a haughty scowl, and appear to be perfect, it angers those we disagree with and prevents them from hearing a word we say. No one believes we are perfect anyway, so when we act like we've never messed up, it creates a barrier.

Authenticity and empathy draw people in.

11. **Cut the sarcasm.**

Sarcasm is defined as the use of irony to mock or convey contempt. While modern generations use sarcasm frequently and flippantly, it is not helpful or funny when discussing a serious topic like abortion. Those we are talking with may not understand the sarcastic undertones in our voices, which could cause them to believe we are hardened, bitter, or judgmental.

One specific example is referring to an abortion clinic as a "mill." There is a definite connection between a mill and an abortion facility but calling it that pushes those who have had abortions and those who work in the industry further away. We must remember that the world views an abortion clinic as a medical facility and although we know the truth, calling it a mill comes across as judgmental, haughty, and contemptuous.

Sarcasm never extends a warm welcome and does not cause people to feel they can safely have a discussion with us.

12. **Reclaim and reframe adoption as the heroic choice.**

As discussed previously, adoption has gotten a bad reputation over the years. It's true, the system is broken in some ways and there have been bad experiences for adoptive parents, adopted children, and birth parents. But the fact that the system is flawed and there are negative stories, does not make abortion a better choice.

As pro-life advocates, we need to educate ourselves about all the positive aspects of adoption. We should be familiar with open adoption and be able to express the beauty of the birth mother playing a significant role in the process. There are also many wonderful adoption stories we need to be aware of and share with others. If we begin talking about adoption in a positive light, it will help alter the view so many have on this topic.

13. Dispel lies in love.

Abortion is wrapped up in countless lies and a multitude of misinformation. The abortion industry can be vague and often keeps people in the dark about this topic, but this is also a tactic used by our adversary, Satan.

When we discuss abortion, it's important for us to be mindful of the lies people have believed about the topic, to seek out truthful responses to these lies, and dispel them in a loving way. Simply telling someone what they believe is wrong, isn't beneficial. We must do our homework and be kind as we redirect misguided beliefs. No one likes to be told they're wrong and if we're hateful and disrespectful, they will discount everything we say. But if we are gentle, kind, and respectful, people are more likely to listen and possibly change their point of view.

How to Communicate with Abortion-Vulnerable Women

If you serve on the front lines in the fight against abortion, I want to say thank you for your willingness to obey God's call. I know from personal experience this type of service is often unappreciated and can be discouraging, but this work is crucial. Sidewalk advocates and pregnancy resource centers are often the only thing standing between an abortion-vulnerable woman and the choice to end her child's life. We are unveiling truth in a culture of lies. We are the last hope for the babies within these women's wombs. These babies deserve for us to make the very best attempt to save their lives.

The abortion industry claims to care for these women, to serve them without judgement, and to solve their problem. If we desire for abortion-vulnerable women to give us a chance instead of running to the clinic, we must be intentional with how we treat them.

Words matter. Actions matter.

How would you talk to someone who was about to jump off a bridge? Would you yell hateful comments or judgmental accusations? Would you hold a gory sign depicting someone else who jumped previously? Would you belittle them and glare at them with disdain?

Or would you be cautious, gentle, and kind? Would you stay mindful of how brief the moments you have are and make them count? Would you build them up and remind them there are so many things worth living for?

Being mindful of the tools already listed, here's a few tools for your "*Love Tool Kit.*" These are especially important when talking specifically to abortion-vulnerable women.

1. Pray for wisdom.

I understand that not all pro-life advocates will agree with the tools suggested in this book but it's vital for us all to pray for wisdom concerning the way we treat abortion-vulnerable women.

Proverbs 21:2a (ESV) says, "Every way of a man is right in his own eyes," but God is the only One who can provide discernment for us, regardless of the situation we find ourselves in. Regarding communication with abortion-vulnerable women, instead of simply believing what we think is correct, let's pray for wisdom and guidance as to the way God would have us think, communicate, and interact.

> "For the Lord gives wisdom, from His mouth come knowledge and understanding." Proverbs 2:6 (ESV)

> "But if any of you lacks wisdom, let him ask of God, who gives to all generously and without reproach, and it will be given to him." James 1:5 (ESV)

God knows the heart of the women we are trying to serve, and He knows how best to reach them. We can trust His guidance and the wisdom He offers us.

2. Remember the Golden Rule.

One of the most famous Bible teachings is often referred to as the Golden Rule.

> "Do to others as you would have them do to you." Luke 6:31 (NIV)

This appears to be a simple principle, but it is often difficult to follow through with. Many pro-life individuals find it difficult to imagine themselves in the same predicament an abortion-vulnerable woman is in. But I assure you, most of these women never imagined they would end up at the abortion clinic either. We must be empathetic towards these ladies and put ourselves in their shoes. Doing so will allow us to determine how we would want to be treated if we were going through the same thing. If we wouldn't want to be yelled at, we shouldn't yell at them. If we wouldn't want someone to glare hatefully at us, we shouldn't do that to them. If we wouldn't want to read a sign that called us a murderer, then we shouldn't hold those signs up for them to see.

It's a simple rule. Treat others the way you want to be treated. This pertains to everyone, even those considering abortion. These are God's precious ones, whether they know it or not. Are we treating them the way we would want to be treated?

3. **Be aware of the plank in our own eyes.**

> "Do not judge, or you too will be judged. For in the same way you judge others, you will be judged, and with the measure you use, it will be measured to you. Why do you look at the speck of sawdust in your brother's eye and pay no attention to the plank in your own eye? How can you say to your brother, 'Let me take the speck out of your eye,' when all the time there is a plank in your own eye? You hypocrite, first take the plank out of your own eye, and then you will see clearly to remove the speck from your brother's eye."
> Matthew 7:1–5 (NIV)

These words were spoken by Jesus. He was reminding His followers how hypocritical and dangerous it is to judge others. The reminder is for us as well.

We are all sinners. Period.

As discussed previously, God does not view one sin as worse than another. So, who are we to judge the abortion-vulnerable woman? If we want to make a positive impact, we must be aware of the "plank in our own eyes" and turn away from a judgmental, hateful postures. There's no doubt about it, abortion-vulnerable women will pick up on critical, haughty attitudes and any attempt to help them will be fruitless.

4. **Remind ourselves who these women are.**

The babies we are hoping to save from abortion are made in the image of God. We must remind ourselves that their mothers are too. The loss of hope these women feel does not change the plans God has for them or how He feels about them.

Both mother and child matter to God, so they should both matter to us.

If we want to save the life of the baby, we must first save the woman carrying it.

In chapter 5 we discussed, in detail, who the abortion-vulnerable woman is, what she is enduring, and why she may be considering abortion. When we lose sight of the humanity of these women or the forget how real their crisis is to them, I believe rereading that chapter will be beneficial. We should also ask God to help us remain mindful of the truth about those we're observing, so that our compassion for them will trump our frustrations and cause us to treat them with gentleness and grace.

5. **Consider how others perceive love.**

I believe serving as a sidewalk advocate or in a pregnancy resource center is God's work because God is pro-life. He places men and women on the front lines to help save the women and babies entering the abortion clinics. Receiving this calling does not negate our command to love others. People perceive love differently and we need to remember that. If we are called to love the women entering an abortion clinic, we need to ask ourselves if they are perceiving our words and behavior as love. Someone may think yelling the truth about abortion is loving, but I guarantee the woman being screamed at does not perceive it that way. Signs with horrific pictures and unloving comments are also never perceived as loving.

If it's our goal to ultimately save the life of a child, we must consider how the mother will perceive our approach to help her. If something we say or do would keep her from believing we love her and her child, then we probably shouldn't do it.

6. **Win her trust.**

The abortion industry is bold, loud, and fearless. They say and do whatever necessary to persuade women to choose abortion. The way we talk about abortion and the way we treat those considering abortion, are our opportunities to win the trust of those who need our help. Aiming to win the trust of someone will greatly impact our words and actions. When has yelling, being hypocritical, belittling others, and pointing fingers ever earned someone's trust? The answer is, never.

Consider salt and sugar. They look the same. They both have good intentions too, to flavor our food. However, salt and sugar taste quite different. The same is true for those of us in the pro-life movement. We all believe in the sanctity of life and have the same goal in mind, to save lives. We all have good intentions, but we do not all taste the same. Some of us cause a bitter taste in the mouth of an abortion-vulnerable woman, while others cause a sweet taste. Bitterness will cause her to flee. Sweetness will cause her to trust.

The baby automatically comes along with the mom when we earn her trust.

7. **Stay calm.**

Abortion is a life-or-death issue. Those serving on the front lines often feel the pressure building and, at times, their anxiety begins to take over. It's easy to get frustrated, upset, and angry. Even in those moments, we must stay calm. Our raised voices, rushed actions, and irritated attitudes will not help the situation.

The way many people share their opinions could easily be compared to a fire hose. Imagine someone pointing that hose at your face and bombarding with you water. Even if you were thirsty, it wouldn't be helpful, would it? The same is true with our thoughts and ideas about abortion, even when we mean well. If the way we talk to abortion-vulnerable women resembles a forceful blast of water, we need to reevaluate. Sharing what we have to offer them, like a gentle stream and in a calm manner, will always be the better option.

8. **Don't worry about being right.**

This tool may be disliked by some, but I encourage you to truly consider the impact it could have. When a woman is about to walk into an abortion clinic or when she walks into a pregnancy center, she is on the brink of what could be the worst decision of her life. She is broken, tired, scared, and often misled. This is not the time to be pushy. In these moments, it's not as important to be right as it is to be kind and gentle.

The moments we have with her are brief and the way we make her feel will cause her to trust us or cause her to run even faster into the clinic.

Sharing our opinions is acceptable but pushing our opinions on the abortion-vulnerable is selfish and places our desire to be right above the needs of the women we're trying to serve. It's okay if she doesn't agree with us or consider us wise. We aren't trying to win an argument; we're trying to save a life.

Jesus was always right, but He did not shove it down the throat of others. He was gentle, kind, loving, honest, and patient. Those qualities caused people to listen to Him and to trust Him. The same could be true for us.

9. **Lay down the signs.**

This is another controversial tool, I'm sure. But as a woman who has been both abortion-vulnerable and post-abortive, I want to share how condemning the signs appear. When women are driving toward an abortion clinic and see the signs from a distance, they assume whoever is holding them are judgmental, hateful protestors. The clinic staff has already warned these women about sidewalk advocates and has told them they should avoid the advocates at all costs. The media also portrays all sidewalk advocates as violent, hateful protestors. Therefore, I believe the signs do more harm than good.

Not all signs are bad. Some are necessary. For example, signs containing the information for a pregnancy resource center or the website for Abortion Pill Reversal are very helpful. Signs that say, "you are loved," "I regret my abortion," or "we're here to help" can also be beneficial. Signs of any kind are most beneficial when placed in the ground, however, because holding a sign places a barrier between a sidewalk advocate and the woman he's trying to help. A smiling, gentle person standing beside a sign that offers help is much more inviting than a person holding a sign, wouldn't you agree?

It's important for us to consider if signs are truly helping our cause, especially when signs contain disgusting photos or hateful slogans. Even informational signs, when seen from a distance, often causes a woman to believe the worst about the person holding it. Signs also put up a physical barrier.

We must keep our focus on the true reason we are standing on the sidewalk. We are not there to make our stance known. We are there to save a baby and a mother from the tragedy of abortion.

10. Remember her rights.

My prayer is that abortion will one day be illegal and unthinkable but for now, we must remind ourselves that the women considering abortion and those walking through the clinic doors, are not doing anything illegal. It's awful but the truth is, in eight states and in Washington, DC, women have the legal right to abort their babies in all nine months of pregnancy. This fact is also one of the many justifications an abortion—vulnerable woman tells herself, attempting to make herself feel better about the choice.

11. Empower her.

The abortion industry and pro-abortion advocates claim that abortion is empowering because it allows women to choose when they will be mothers, therefore giving them control over their lives. That is a false narrative which has blinded so many. Killing our children is not empowering. Being filled with regret and shame is not empowering. Constantly trying to justify our choice and avoiding our emotions is not empowering.

If we are going to demolish this lie, we must empower those women who believe abortion is the best choice. We must remind her that she is strong and capable, that a baby will not be the end of her life, and that there is help available. We must also pray for her and ask God to give her the peace that surpasses all understanding (Philippians 4:7 NIV) so that she is able to pause and see clearly, long enough to hear and believe the truth.

12. Embrace the battle.

We are in a difficult battle against abortion, there's no doubt about it. We must remember, we win in the end.

"With God on our side we will win; He will defeat our enemies."
Psalm 108:13 (GNT)

"Let us not become weary in doing good, for at the proper time we will reap a harvest, if we do not give up." Galatians 6:9 (NIV)

I encourage each of you to embrace the battle you have been chosen to fight. Run toward the fire because we cannot fight or rescue from a distance. Do not give up or let discouragement overtake you. This is a battle worth fighting and God is on our side!

How to Communicate with a Post-Abortive Woman

As discussed in chapter 6, those who have experienced abortion have endured so much more than most people realize. The physical and emotional trauma that occurs during an abortion procedure are extremely damaging and in the years that follow, their emotions often become like a prison. Most women hide what they've done, try to deal with the trauma they've endured on their own, and are covered with shame for years and years. So many of the post-abortive women believe they deserve to live a life of fear, guilt, shame, and self-loathing because they had an abortion. I refer to post-abortive women, but the truth is, many men who have an aborted child feel the same way.

God has good, good plans for each of His children. Satan wants to put an end to those plans and rob us of the blessings God has for us. Abortion is the perfect tool for our enemy. He uses it to tear us away from God's plans and cause us to believe the worst about ourselves. Because of our abortions, he whispers lies that result in us believing that we are unlovable, unforgiveable, and unworthy of anything good in life.

Although there are countless stories with the potential to change our generation's opinion about abortion, most post-abortive women never talk about their abortions. They would never do it again and wish wholeheartedly that they had made a different choice, but they are scared to admit their abortions out loud. They could expose the truth about this so-called empowering option, but they have remained silenced.

If we want to put an end to abortion, it is imperative that we become intentional with our words and actions regarding those who have experienced the tragedy of abortion.

The tools we've already discussed still apply along with a few additional tools for your "*Love Tool Kit.*" These are specifically for discussions with men and women who have experienced abortion.

1. **Love and accept her.**

   When a woman finally comes out of hiding after an abortion, it's often because she feels like she's drowning in sorrow. She's probably tried everything else, but nothing has helped her. Sometimes, a therapist or counselor has helped her discover that her abortion is the root of so many of her issues. It is rare that a post-abortive woman decides to talk about her abortion for no reason. It's a big deal for these ladies to begin a healing journey and it is not easy. Whether it's been two weeks or forty-two years, finding healing after abortion is extremely difficult. The result, however, is worth every tear, every sleepless night, and every prayer.

If you are blessed with the opportunity to minister to someone wounded by abortion, consider it an honor, because so many women will not tell anyone. Showing her love and acceptance even though she made the choice to abort, will be a game changer for her. If she can believe she is loveable and that someone accepts her, even though she had an abortion, she can start believing the many necessary things for healing to occur.

2. Acknowledge the trauma and encourage healing.

We previously covered the trauma of abortion in detail, but this cannot be stressed enough. Women who have undergone an abortion of any kind have experienced something extremely traumatic. This trauma should be treated just like any other trauma and taken seriously, but it rarely is. Most women never deal with it which often results in Post-Abortion Stress Syndrome. As pro-life advocates, we need to advocate for healing in the lives of these women.

Encouraging women (and men) to talk about their abortions, to join support groups, and/or engage in a post-abortion Bible study is vital. Most women who have dealt with this nightmare, will only talk to others who have experienced it too. As more post-abortive people talk about what they've endured, more and more will realize it's safe for them to come out of hiding as well.

3. Be patient.

Many pro-life individuals simply cannot understand why someone who knows the tragedy of abortion doesn't just speak up and expose the truth about it. We should all consider a time in our own lives when we messed up and regretted our actions. It isn't easy to talk about things we regret. We usually don't want to share it with others either. Now, imagine what you did was the most controversial topic of our generation and laced with judgmental, hateful people pointing fingers. That would make it even more difficult to talk about, right?

Covering up sin is not a new concept. We have all tried to cover up sin at some point. Even Adam and Eve tried to hide from God when they sinned in the Garden of Eden. (Genesis 3:7–10 NIV) So we shouldn't be surprised that women try to cover up abortion.

Most of these women have desperately tried to hide their abortions because they fear what others would say and how they would be treated. It may take some time for women to begin trusting again. It may be a while before many of them feel comfortable discussing this topic with anyone. When a post-abortive woman is ready, we must be there to love her well and help her along on her healing journey. Doing so will be a blessing to her, but also to the pro-life movement.

4. **Extend grace.**

Shame is very heavy, but grace outweighs it every time. Even though she's made a terrible choice, even those she's hidden it from everyone, even though she is in a pit of depression, even though she doesn't deserve it, we must extend grace to her.

> "For there is no distinction: for all have sinned and fall short of the glory of God." Romans 3:23 (ESV)

> "For the grace of God has been revealed, bringing salvation to all people." Titus 2:11 (NLT)

God has shown grace to us; therefore, I believe it's time for all of us to show grace to those who have experienced the tragedy of abortion.

5. **Bring peace.**

We are called to be peacemakers, but I believe we're also called to be peace-bringers. When we are filled with the Holy Spirit, He produces the fruits of the Spirit within us. (Galatians 5:23 NIV) One of those fruits is peace. So, when we are discussing abortion or talking to someone who has had an abortion, we should bring peace.

There is a war ensuing within her. She needs peace but fears the worst. Determine to bring the peace of God with you into conversations about abortion so that post-abortive men and women can experience it and believe it exists for them.

6. **Understand that shaming to repentance is fruitless.**

It's tempting to call out the sin of others. It's also easy to point fingers at others instead of showing grace and compassion. Doing this, however, is harmful in most situations. Whether we're discussing abortion in general or talking directly to someone who has had an abortion, shaming her is not beneficial. Some believe shaming someone will cause them to repent of their sin, but in reality, it causes women to run as quick as they can into a clinic, and it motivates post-abortive women to hide. It has also been known to cause some women to attempt suicide.

To have the greatest, positive impact in the fight against abortion, we must stop shaming those who have had abortions so they will feel comfortable enough to come out of hiding, find healing, and share their stories.

9

Time for Change is Now

IT'S MY FIRM BELIEF that all of God's children were created on purpose, for a purpose. For many of us, that involves fighting against abortion. If you have ever served in the pro-life movement, I applaud you. Thank you for your willingness to speak up for those who cannot speak for themselves. There is no doubt about it, the work you've done and continue to do, is God's work!

> "Speak up for those who cannot speak for themselves; ensure justice for those being crushed. Yes, speak up for the poor and helpless, and see that they get justice." Proverbs 31:8–10 (NLT)

There are numerous pro-life advocates who have been serving for many, many years. I know sometimes it can feel difficult to change the way we do things, but there has never been a better time to reconsider our approach. It's important not to make "the way we've always done things," become sacred. Life refuses to remain static; it refuses to remain the same. We must change too, because whether we like it or not, many of the methods of yesterday are not appropriate for today or tomorrow.

God wants to cultivate each of our lives and weed out the things that shouldn't be there. This will help us grow into who He designed us to be and therefore, we will be able to fulfill the good works He designed us for. But we must be willing to allow Him to do so.

> "We have become his poetry, a re-created people that will fulfill the destiny he has given each of us, for we are joined to Jesus, the Anointed One. Even before we were born, God planned our

destiny and the good works we would do to fulfill it!" Ephesians 2:10 (TPT)

Recently, I posted a graphic on social media giving the details of an upcoming post-abortion Bible study. Someone commented, saying she would never talk about her abortion with a religious person because, according to her, religion and abortion obviously do not go together. I shared my story with her and explained how Jesus had taken the shame of my past and made something beautiful from it. As we typed back and forth, it became clear, she had only heard sarcastic, mean-spirited, judgmental comments about abortion from those she viewed as religious. She couldn't believe that someone who loved Jesus would ever want to help her find healing or that it was possible for them to love her without judgement.

This generation is hungry, but they have little interest in religion. They are looking for something real. They are looking for hope! As Christ followers, we have exactly what they need, but for us to point these precious people toward truth and help them find what they're seeking, we need to lay down the way we've always done things.

The message will not change but the tools must.

It's my prayer that *Lead with Love* has provided new insight on this topic and that all readers will grasp the importance of the post-abortive woman in the fight for life. I believe if the tools provided within these pages are implemented, the pro-life "team" will become one that is welcoming and inviting to its most valuable players—-those who have experienced the tragedy of abortion and can best expose the ugly truth about it.

> *Our willingness to imitate Jesus in every way, to speak the truth in love, and to allow compassion to trump judgement, will be a launching pad for a much-needed, wonderful shift in the fight against abortion.*

In many ways, the post-abortive man and woman have been silenced in the war against abortion. Imagine for a moment how powerful it would be for them to rise out of the ashes of their past and join us in the fight for life. The impact they would have is unquantifiable.

Change is often difficult, which causes people to shy away from it. Difficulty, however, is not a satisfactory reason to stay the same. After all, many wonderful things in life are challenging. I believe it's time for the pro-life community to do what it's never done before and make a greater impact than it's ever made before. Doing so will require letting go of our old way of doing things. The future of the pro-life movement, as well as the future of countless lives, depends on what we choose to do now. If transformation begins today, it will impact so many tomorrows.

It may take some time for the changes to become apparent on a large scale. That's okay. God-sized dreams often take more than one generation. Don't get discouraged if the pace feels slow at first, just keep moving in the right direction. The direction we're headed in is much more important than our speed. Our willingness to imitate Jesus in every way, to speak the truth in love, and to allow compassion to trump judgment, will be a launching pad for a much-needed, wonderful shift in the fight against abortion.

In Conclusion

Throughout the pages of this book, the issues that have damaged the fight for life have been exposed, insight on how to turn things around has been shared, and advice on how to discuss the topic of abortion has been given. We hope that respectful and loving techniques have been learned for communicating with someone who has an abortion in their past and how to minister to someone considering abortion.

I hope you feel the magnitude of this issue and that your passion and dedication in the fight for life has been renewed and rejuvenated.

I pray that you understand the impact for life that is possible if we, the pro-life movement, embrace a Christ-like approach in this fight. With this strategy, we will see the truth about abortion being exposed, lives being saved, and women finding healing after abortion. The cycle will be broken when the warriors for life seek God's help and love others well; even those who have had abortions and those considering one.

> "For when you demonstrate the same love I have for you by loving one another, everyone will know that you're my true followers."
> John 13:35 (TPT)

Jesus clearly stated how the world would recognize His followers. They will not know us by our accusations, judgmental stances, hypocrisy, divisiveness, unkind social media posts, political outbursts, gossip sessions, or haughty attitudes.

They will identify us as Jesus' followers, by the love we show them.

When our greatest attribute is love, we can be sure that others will know we belong to Jesus. Our love will encourage people to discover Him for themselves. With our love, families will find healing after abortion, and women will choose life for their children. The stakes are too high for our motives to be confused with anything other than love.

It's not only vital that others see Jesus in us, but also that we remember we are warriors in the Lord's army. As soldiers of Christ in this fight, we must take up the whole armor of God to overcome the enemy.

The war against abortion is often complex and burdensome. It can feel like an impossible, uphill battle. It's not a fight that will be won overnight or with ease but with love, darkness will flee, truth will be received, freedom will be experienced, and lives will be saved.

Take heart, fellow Warrior, we will behold triumph when we lead with love!

Epilogue

LAURA VISITED HER MOTHER often as the cancer aggressively took over her body. Each day seemed worse than the day before. Laura had been trying to process the secret her mother had shared a few weeks earlier. Although she didn't want to feel anger toward her mother, some very difficult emotions emerged after learning that she had a sibling, who had been aborted. She couldn't understand why her mother hadn't told her the truth about abortion when Laura asked. She kept wondering what would have happened if her mother had been honest about her story, instead of hiding it for so long.

Laura's mother regretted telling her daughter the truth because she could sense the resentment and disappointment it had caused. Now, at the end of her life, she guessed her daughter probably hated her because of the secret, hidden for so long.

Laura was struggling with another thought, however. She was trying to decide if she should tell her mom that she, too, had experienced abortion. Her husband was the only person she had ever told, and while he was accepting and loving, they had never talked about it again. The mere idea of saying the words out loud caused anxiety to form in the pit of her stomach. Her mother was deteriorating quickly, which meant her time was limited. If Laura was going to share her secret with her mother, she needed to do it soon.

One evening, while driving to see her mother, Laura decided it was time to share her story. Her mother was alert and easy to talk to that evening, so Laura began speaking about the one thing she never, ever wanted her mom to know. She explained the circumstances she had been in when she found out about the pregnancy. She told her about the protestors and the horrific procedure she endured. She disclosed the fear, shame, and regret that had kept her silent for so long, just as her mother had done.

Both women cried as Laura recounted her abortion and all that had followed it. The conversation continued with questions being answered and "what-ifs" being shared. Laura climbed onto the bed and snuggled up to her mom, while they both wept for the children they had never been able to meet.

As Laura prepared to go home, her mother begged her not to continue hiding her abortion. She didn't want her daughter to come to the end of her life and realize the abortion not only took the life of a child, but it also resulted in an unfulfilled life of her own. Her mother understood that feeling well. Laura said she would search for resources and try to find healing. Her mother sighed in relief. Then she said, "Soon I'll be able to hold both of our precious babies in Heaven. Oh, what a joyful day that will be." With tears in her eyes, Laura kissed her mother on the cheek and said, "Bye, Mom, I love you so much."

The next morning, Laura discovered that her mother had passed away in her sleep. Even though she had known this day was coming, the news caused an unfamiliar, deep sadness to well up within her. Then, she remembered the beautiful moments she had spent with her mother the night before. Her heart became filled with gratitude for the closeness and healing their discussion had brought about.

In the weeks to come, as Laura grieved the loss of her mother, she couldn't escape the vision of her mother sitting in a rocking chair, gently rocking two adorable babies. She knew her mother was at peace and full of joy. She was with the child she had aborted, and her grandchild that Laura had aborted. This image brought comfort to Laura's heart. She was also constantly reminded of the promise she had made her mother. She knew she needed to seek out resources for someone filled with regret and shame because of an abortion.

As she searched online, Laura was surprised by the books, Bible studies, and support groups available for women who had been wounded by abortion. She had assumed the resources would be very limited. After ordering a couple of books to read, she signed up for an online Bible study. Laura began counting down the days until the Bible study began and she was terrified, but she knew this was a first step in the right direction.

Laura had almost talked herself out of joining the online group, but she kept hearing her mom's voice, encouraging her to find healing. So, she joined the call and tiptoed through the first session. As the weeks went by, she heard the stories of other women and realized she wasn't alone in her experience: her emotions, ways of coping, shame, or her desire to stay hidden.

Things began to change for Laura when she decided to fully accept God's forgiveness and forgive herself. The transformation occurring within her heart because of this group of women, and the time they spent studying God's Word, was unbelievable. Her husband and children were amazed by the changes they saw in her. She began to experience life in a new way and felt free for the first time, as an adult.

Laura's decision to find healing was like a line drawn in the sand. She had allowed God to heal her heart and the bondage she had previously experienced, was eradicated. She was made new. A desire to help other women began to well up within her. She realized she wasn't afraid any longer and decided it was time to tell her children about the abortion and the missing sibling in their family.

Laura's daughters were twelve and fourteen when their mother sat them down and shared the secret that she had been keeping for most of her life. The girls were shocked by the news but could see the sadness in their mother's eyes; a sadness that had been caused by her choice to abort. They were thankful she had told them, even though they couldn't believe they had sibling they would never know. As they listened and watched the tears stream down their mom's face, the truth about abortion solidified in their minds. Neither girl had much of an opinion about the topic previously, but after hearing their mom's story, they knew abortion was not only wrong, but it was also devastating for women who chose it.

As the girls grew up, they talked openly with Laura about hard topics like abortion, sex, pornography, sex-trafficking, rape, etc. They knew their mom wouldn't judge them because of their questions. She had always made it clear, she wanted them to feel completely free to talk to her. She didn't want them to travel down the same road she had.

Through the years, Laura volunteered as a sidewalk advocate outside of the very same clinic, she had entered so many years before. As women drove into the parking lot, she smiled at them sweetly, offered them literature, and when given the opportunity, she shared her story with them. She also encouraged her fellow advocates to lay down their signs, put the bullhorns away, and speak with love and kindness. The other advocates agreed to do so after Laura explained how the condemning protestors and graphic signs had only pushed her through the clinic doors more quickly.

Once the advocates modified their approach on the sidewalk, they noticed more and more women were willing to talk with them. When Laura, or any other post-abortive woman served on the sidewalk, the other advocates encouraged them to share their experiences during and after abortion. The first-hand experience a post-abortive person could offer often opened the eyes of the abortion-vulnerable women they encountered, causing them to choose life.

When Laura's oldest daughter, Sabrina, was in college, she met a young man, who swept her off her feet. She had avoided romantic relationships previously because she desired to stay pure for the man she would marry. Her parents had always stressed the importance of purity and encouraged dating to be taken seriously, as the path to find her future husband. Sabrina had listened closely to her mother's warnings about sex before marriage and the abortions that often followed. She had friendships with boys in high school but none of them ever seemed like someone she'd want to marry. When she met this young man on her college campus however, she felt God nudging her and she knew there was something special about him. The two got close but she desired to wait until they were married to have sex, and her boyfriend agreed.

Right before Sabrina's senior year of college, the man of her dreams proposed. Laura helped her daughter plan a beautiful wedding that took place a couple of weeks after graduation. It wasn't easy, but Sabrina and her fiancé waited until their wedding night to be sexually intimate, and it was the sweetest of experiences for them both. Knowing her mother's story had helped Sabrina remain pure and encouraged her to avoid so many costly situations, which blessed Laura tremendously.

Laura's younger daughter, Molly, had not been as determined to remain pure until marriage, even though she believed it was best route to take. She had dated several boys in high school but once in college, she became sexually active.

Right after Sabrina's wedding, Molly discovered she was pregnant. As soon as she found out, she decided to talk to her mom. In fact, her mom was the first and only person she wanted to talk to, so she drove home the same day. Laura was surprised by her daughter's unexpected visit but as soon as she saw Molly's face, she knew exactly what was going on. She saw that familiar fear and shame in her daughter's eyes. Laura had experienced the same emotions when she found out about her own pregnancy at nineteen.

Laura grabbed Molly and squeezed her tight, and the two cried together. No words were spoken until Laura finally asked, "How far along are you?" Molly wasn't sure but she knew it had been about two months since her last period. The two ladies sat together and talked about the crisis Molly faced.

Molly told her mother, "I can understand now why some women choose abortion. It seems like the easy way out of this mess. It feels like the pro-choice advocates really care about me. At least I don't have to worry about them judging me. On the other hand, there's no way I would seek help from those pro-life groups because they are so judgmental and rude. Making this problem disappear seems like the best choice since I'm a single college student with no money." She looked at her shoes and shrugged, "But I can't even contemplate abortion as an option because I know how much it hurt you. And I know how much it hurt me to find out about the sibling I'll never meet. I don't know what I'm going to do but I know I cannot have an abortion."

Tears continued to stream down her face as she mourned the life and dreams, she believed this baby would eilliminate. Laura smiled at her daughter and said, "Don't you worry. You are strong and your family will be here for you every step of the way. You may need to move home and attend a nearby college, but all your dreams and goals can still be achieved. You'll just have a little one cheering for you instead of a shroud of shame and regret."

About seven months later, Molly gave birth to a breath-taking little girl. Laura had been in the room as her granddaughter entered the world and she experienced God's presence strongly. She knew her Heavenly Father had brought her full circle, allowing her to witness a shift in her family line; a shift that had materialized because of her willingness to share her abortion story with her daughters.

Molly snuggled the newborn close for the first time, and then handed the bundle to her mom saying, "I want you to meet Elizabeth Rose." Laura couldn't believe her ears. She was overwhelmed with joy and excitement as she rocked her first grandchild. This precious baby had been given the perfect name; a name that had first belonged to her great-grandmother.

Laura's story helped save many preborn babies from abortion over the years. The child she held in her arms may have also been aborted if not for Laura's mother, Rose, speaking up about her own abortion at the end of her life. Her story led to Laura's healing, which allowed her to boldly share her experience with her daughters and so many others. Laura's openness exposed the truth about abortion and made it impossible for Molly to even consider aborting her child.

A few months later, Laura took her daughters to place flowers on their grandmother's grave. Elizabeth Rose joined them. As they stood there, it occurred to them that four generations of women in their family were represented. Tears trickled down their faces as they imagined how different things could be, for all of them, if Grandma Rose had let her secret die with her. They prayed and praised God for the beautiful blessings He had birthed through Grandma Rose's vulnerability and Laura's boldness.

Imagine how different things could be for women and babies everywhere, if those who know the tragedy of abortion felt safe enough to come out of hiding, accepted enough to speak up, and free enough to boldly expose the darkness.

Imagine what could happen if we lead with love.

Note from the Author

IF YOU HAVE EXPERIENCED abortion, you can most likely relate to many of the things shared in this book. I know coming out of hiding seems terrifying. I know you've felt judged and unwelcome in the fight against abortion. I know you have tried your best to forget what you've done but the pain just won't go away. I know the darkness seems safer than the light. I chose to write this book because I understand, firsthand how you feel, but I've also learned that our stories are vital in the fight for life.

It's my desire that the words written here will be a catalyst for change in the pro-life movement. I believe God has so much in store! If you regret your choice to abort or if you wish you could help other women make a different choice, I encourage you to come out of hiding and allow God to heal your heart. He can do things in your life and through your story that you cannot even imagine!

> "Now to him who is able to do immeasurably more than all we ask or imagine, according to his power that is at work within us, to him be glory in the church and in Christ Jesus throughout all generations, for ever and ever! Amen." Ephesians 3:20–21 (NIV)

As the pro-life movement begins to see the value in our stories and becomes more welcoming and loving toward us, I pray you will receive their invitation. That is frightening, I know. The judgement, fear, rejection, and shame we've all felt in response to many pro-life messages and advocates is real, but we must extend grace to them as well.

We are the greatest weapon in the fight against abortion because our firsthand experiences will expose the truth about abortion and light up the darkness. We've been silent far too long, but God will honor our willingness to speak up so that others aren't fooled the way we were. He will bless our efforts and give us the strength we need. When we slip out from behind the shadows and courageously fight for life, the healing we'll experience will be extraordinary.

Sweet Friend, God desires freedom for you. He also wants to use your past experiences to help someone else find that same freedom and prevent another from ever being chained by shame and guilt, like we were.

> "He always comes alongside us to comfort us in every suffering so that we can come alongside those who are in any painful trial. We can bring them this same comfort that God has poured out upon us." 2 Corinthians 2:14 (TPT)

The time has come to exchange beauty for ashes. It may not be easy, but we promise it will be worth it.

By His Grace,

Tori

 For more information about Not Forgotten Ministries please visit our website www.theyarenotforgotten.com

Bibliography

"Abortion Procedures: What You Need to Know." AbortionProcedures.com. https://www.abortionprocedures.com (2021)

Biggs, Antonia, Gould, Heather & Foster, Diana Greene. "Understanding Why Women Seek abortions in the US." *BMC Women's Health* 13, 29. https://doi.org/10.1186/1472-6874-13-29 (2013, July 5).

"Christianity in the United States." Wikipedia. https://en.wikipedia.org/w/index.php?title=Christianity_in_the_United_States&oldid=1066961893 (2022, January 21).

Coleman, Priscilla, Boswell, Kaitlyn, Etzkorn, Katrina, & Turnwald, Rachel. "Women Who Suffered Emotionally from Abortion: A Qualitative Synthesis of Their Experiences." *Journal of American Physicians and Surgeons Volume 22 Number 4.* https://www.jpands.org/vol22no4/coleman.pdf (2017, Winter)

Green, Lisa. New Survey: Women Go Silently from Church to Abortion Clinic. https://www.care-net.org/churches-blog/new-survey-women-go-silently-from-church-to-abortion-clinic (2015, Nov 23)

Ireland, Luu. Who Chooses Abortion? More Women Than You Might Think. https://theconversation.com/who-chooses-abortion-more-women-than-you-might-think-99982 (2018, July 27).

Jefferson, Thomas. "Declaration of Independence." https://www.archives.gov/founding-docs/declaration (et al, 1776, July 4).

Shaw, Tori. "Kristen Experienced Physical and Emotional 'Agony' After Taking the Abortion Pill." https://www.liveaction.org/news/kristen-physical-emotional-pain-abortion-pill/ (2021, July 23).

Shaw, Tori. "Pregnant Again After an Abortion, Kara Found the Support She Needed to Fight for Her Daughter." https://www.liveaction.org/news/pregnant-after-abortion-kara-support-fight-daughter/ (2021, November 2).

Sullins, Paul. "Aborting the Wanted Child." https://www.thepublicdiscourse.com/2020/01/59909/ (2020, January 22).

"The Pro-Life Reply to: 'Women Will Die from Illegal Abortions.'" Live Action. https://prolifereplies.liveaction.org/back-alley/ (2019, June 25).

"U.S Abortion Statistics." Abort73. https://abort73.com/abortion_facts/us_abortion_statistics/ (2021)